Cycle of Rebirth
From Emotional Release to Spiritual Awakening
By Lily Cooper

Copyright © 2023 Luiz Santos
All rights reserved. No part of this book may be reproduced in any form or by any means without written permission from the copyright holder.
Cover image © Vellaz Studio
Review by Armando Vellaz
Graphic design by Amadeu Brumm
Layout by Matheus Costa
All rights reserved to:
Luiz A. Santos
Category: Mythology / Ancient History

Summary

- Prologue 5
- Chapter 1 Liberation and Rebirth 7
- Chapter 2 Preparation 12
- Chapter 3 Meditation and Breathing Techniques 17
- Chapter 4 Identifying and Releasing Emotional Blockages 22
- Chapter 5 Fundamental Liberation Practices 27
- Chapter 6 Connection with the Inner Self 33
- Chapter 7 Trauma and Energetic Imprints 39
- Chapter 8 Holotropic Breathing 45
- Chapter 9 Overcoming Limiting Mental Patterns 52
- Chapter 10 Somatic Integration in Rituals 59
- Chapter 11 Stages of Emotional Healing 66
- Chapter 12 Therapeutic Guidance 72
- Chapter 13 Higher Self and Inner Wisdom 79
- Chapter 14 Subconscious Memories and Personal Archetypes . 86
- Chapter 15 Energy Purification and Cleansing 93
- Chapter 16 Chakras and Energy Centers 100
- Chapter 17 Other Rebirth Rituals 107
- Chapter 18 Dreams and Symbolism 114
- Chapter 19 Therapeutic Process 122
- Chapter 20 Artistic Expression 129
- Chapter 21 Personal Boundaries and Overcoming .. 137
- Chapter 22 Building a New Identity 145
- Chapter 23 Practical Application 151
- Chapter 24 Integration of Transformation 157
- Chapter 25 Reinforcing Identity and Confidence 163

Chapter 26 Self-Compassion Practices 167
Chapter 27 Cultivating Gratitude 171
Chapter 28 Intentions for the Future 176
Chapter 29 Continuous Growth Cycle 182
Chapter 30 Others on the Path to Rebirth 189
Chapter 31 Rebirth Cycle 196
Epilogue 202

Prologue

You, who now hold this book in your hands, may not yet suspect the potential it holds, the doors it is capable of opening within you. It is no coincidence that your eyes have rested upon these words; there is a silent call that resonates within your soul, a search that has brought you here. This is not an ordinary book, and you are not an ordinary reader. There is something within you that yearns for liberation, that seeks a deeper meaning amidst the layers of your existence.

Within these pages lie ancient secrets, whispers of wisdom that have traversed the ages. But they are not merely stories of distant times; they are codes that speak directly to the most intimate part of you. Each sentence is like a whisper that reverberates in your mind, inviting you to remember something that, perhaps, you have long forgotten. And as you dive into this reading, you will open a path within yourself, a path that will guide you beyond the boundaries of the visible, to the depths where the answers you have always sought reside.

Here, liberation and rebirth are not mere concepts; they are experiences that await you. You will be led to confront the unseen layers that limit you, to perceive the subtle threads that still bind you to pains and fears from a distant past. But, more than that, you will be invited to lift the veil of illusions that you have built to protect yourself. You will set aside the burden you carry, and in doing so, feel the gentle touch of a new awareness, of a freedom that pulses in every cell of your being.

There is no way to predict what you will find along this path. Each chapter is a mirror that reflects aspects of your own journey, a reflection of what lies hidden in your mind and spirit. Do you feel that restlessness moving within your chest? That desire for something more? This is the promise hidden within these lines: the possibility of a rebirth, a renewal that transcends what you imagined to be possible.

But there is a price to pay. It is not a price measured in coins or time, but in courage. The courage to open yourself to the new, to look within and encounter the parts of yourself that you have avoided. Are you capable of looking beyond the surface and recognizing the fragments of your own soul? Are you capable of accepting what you are, without masks, without excuses? If so, then these pages belong to you, for in them you will find what you seek.

You do not need to be an initiate in ancient traditions to understand what is here. Everything you need already resides within you, dormant. This book is merely the key that will awaken what has always been present, but which you perhaps have not dared to explore. With each word, with each concept that you will discover here, you will feel the expansion of your perception, as if a new vision unfolds before your eyes.

And when you reach the end of this book, you will not be the same person who began this journey. Something within you will have changed, even if subtly. The words will not have merely passed through your mind; they will have touched your spirit. Because, deep down, what is revealed here is the very truth of your essence, the reunion with a freedom that has always been yours, but which you now allow yourself to live.

So, proceed. Let these words guide you. Let each page be a portal to a new vision of yourself and of the world. Let this be your moment to cross the boundary between who you were and who you can still become. Because, after all, this journey is yours and yours alone. And what you find within it will be the most intimate and transformative revelation you can experience.

Luiz Santos

Chapter 1
Liberation and Rebirth

The essence of liberation and rebirth therapy is rooted in ancient wisdom, a path woven through ages where seekers yearned to break free from internal constraints and begin anew. At the heart of this therapy lies the holistic vision—a perception of human experience that transcends the physical, piercing into layers of emotion, mind, and spirit. This perspective reminds us that true healing touches not just the tangible body but also the unseen currents of energy that connect us to the world and to ourselves.

The holistic approach, deeply embedded in Eastern and indigenous traditions, stands on the understanding that each being is an intricate tapestry of experiences, memories, energies, and emotions. Every choice, joy, sorrow, and trauma leaves subtle imprints, shaping an internal landscape that can either expand or restrict one's sense of self. As life progresses, many carry an invisible weight, their energies bound to past pains or unfulfilled desires. Liberation therapy, then, serves as an initiation—a sacred unbinding, allowing one to strip away the veils and reconnect with a purer, more authentic essence.

Historically, liberation and rebirth practices can be traced back to ancient rituals that focused on deep purification and symbolic renewal. In the temples of Egypt, initiates would undergo ceremonies meant to sever the ties with their past identities, to emerge cleansed and spiritually awakened. Similarly, shamanic cultures in South America speak of "soul retrieval," a practice to reclaim parts of oneself that may have been lost to trauma or hardship. These traditions, though separated by oceans and eras, share an elemental desire to heal the psyche, spirit, and heart.

In the Eastern traditions, such as in Buddhist and Hindu teachings, practices of rebirth through meditation and breathwork illuminate another layer of liberation. In these cultures, there is an acknowledgment of samsara—the endless cycle of life, death, and rebirth. To be liberated from this cycle, one must break free from attachments and illusions, stepping into a state of higher awareness. Practices in these paths call upon the breath as a central, almost mystical, force—guiding practitioners to cultivate profound mindfulness, to witness and let go of the conditioned responses that bind them.

As the years rolled forward, these practices found new shapes and expressions in modern therapeutic approaches. Figures like Carl Jung explored concepts like the "collective unconscious," drawing from ancient knowledge to unlock new layers of self-discovery within Western psychology. The rise of modern holotropic breathwork and energy-focused therapies, inspired by ancestral methods, has given rebirth and liberation practices a new home in contemporary healing circles. These approaches merge ancient understanding with modern insights, creating a bridge between science and spirituality.

In the realm of rebirth therapy, the act of "letting go" is not merely symbolic—it becomes a ritual of transformation. It calls the individual to recognize the deep imprints left by past experiences and release them with grace, compassion, and purpose. The process of liberation is, in essence, a sacred return, a dismantling of layers that no longer serve, so that one can experience a pure and boundless sense of self.

In its many forms, liberation and rebirth offer profound healing for those who embark on this journey, a way of looking within and embracing the possibility of change. Here, therapy is not only an exercise in self-improvement but a rite, a ceremony through which one dares to confront the deepest recesses of their soul and, by doing so, opens the door to a rebirth unmarred by the shadows of the past.

As liberation and rebirth therapy unfolds, its principles bridge timeless philosophies and modern practices, creating a profound space for transformation. At its core, this journey is a reunion with one's own energy, an opening to release deep-seated patterns and transcend the limits of self-concept. Unlike traditional therapeutic modalities, liberation therapy taps into realms often obscured by daily life—archetypes, inherited beliefs, and spiritual constructs that influence behavior and perception. In this holistic practice, cultural, spiritual, and philosophical elements entwine, drawing from diverse traditions that see the human experience as a blend of the material and the mystical.

The influence of ancient cultures is woven through this therapeutic journey, inviting practitioners to experience release and renewal from different cultural lenses. Indigenous practices of rebirth, from the Amazon to Siberia, incorporate the body, mind, and spirit through ritualistic breathwork, chanting, or sacred plant ceremonies. Each element is intentional, each movement designed to unlock something deep within the psyche, dissolving energetic knots that inhibit personal growth. These cultural lenses, though unique in their expression, point toward a universal truth: the liberation of the spirit is essential to healing, a core tenet that resonates across the human collective.

The modern form of rebirth therapy has evolved to accommodate contemporary lifestyles and the nuanced complexities of modern minds. Here, therapeutic spaces are consciously created to emulate the ancient sacred circles but adapted to provide structure, safety, and accessibility. In these spaces, guided breathing, visualization, and energy-focused exercises invite participants to enter a realm where they might confront and dissolve the inherited imprints and beliefs that shape their lives. This work is deeply personal yet carries echoes of ancient wisdom, reflecting how humanity has always sought to balance the demands of the outer world with the inner self.

Cultural influences on liberation therapy invite practitioners to look beyond personal identities and explore larger, more archetypal narratives. These narratives, which shape the foundation of myths and collective stories, provide a symbolic framework for healing and understanding the self. The archetypes—the Hero, the Shadow, the Nurturer, the Seeker—each hold a mirror to some part of the individual journey, revealing not only personal wounds but also universal patterns and truths. By embodying and exploring these aspects within a therapeutic setting, individuals begin to transcend their specific narratives, finding liberation in the universal and the collective.

Spiritual perspectives within liberation and rebirth therapy invite practitioners to connect with a sense of purpose that transcends individual desires or fears. The influences of Taoist and Zen philosophies, for example, inspire the acceptance of paradox—the recognition that liberation lies not in control but in surrender, not in knowing but in the spaciousness of the unknown. This surrender, however, is not passive; it is a deep, active engagement with life's mysteries and one's inner world, asking participants to trust in the organic unfolding of their journey.

In practice, the fusion of these cultural and spiritual perspectives enables a rebirth experience that is both universal and deeply personal. It becomes an awakening that asks individuals to shed their familiar identities and step into the liminal, a state between the known self and the emergent self. Through breath, movement, visualization, and sacred space, individuals are given the tools to descend into the depths of their consciousness, meeting past versions of themselves, releasing what no longer serves, and embracing what lies beyond.

Modern adaptations of these ancient practices, such as holotropic breathwork, seek to embody these principles while honoring individual limits. Practitioners are guided in a safe, structured setting, using breath as a transformative tool to access expanded states of awareness, where personal insights and profound clarity can emerge. Each breath holds the potential for liberation, a path toward rebirth that awakens dormant energies and allows suppressed emotions to be seen, felt, and ultimately integrated.

In the culmination of each session, the therapeutic process is consciously closed, grounding practitioners in the present while leaving them with a renewed sense of freedom. With each release, the self is reborn, cleansed of energies that once held it captive, and allowed to emerge in alignment with its true essence.

Chapter 2
Preparation

The first steps into liberation and rebirth therapy require intentional preparation, a careful cultivation of mind, body, and environment to open the path toward transformation. This preparation is not simply logistical but is an initiation, a quiet ritual that readies the participant for a journey inward. The physical and energetic surroundings, the mental clarity, and even the physical state of the body are essential components that influence the depth and effectiveness of this practice. Each aspect of preparation aligns with the greater purpose of liberation therapy: to enable release, rebirth, and the emergence of a revitalized self.

The process of physical preparation begins with the body, the vessel through which all experiences are felt, expressed, and processed. It is within the body that memories are stored, where tension and trauma often reside unnoticed. To begin, one is invited to focus on relaxation techniques that soften muscular rigidity and cultivate a state of ease. Gentle stretching, yoga, or mindful movement open the energy channels, creating a flow that loosens stagnant energies and allows the body to become receptive to therapeutic experiences. The more relaxed and attuned the body is, the more it can access its innate wisdom and respond to the deeper workings of liberation therapy.

Alongside physical readiness, psychological preparation forms the second pillar of this journey. The mind, a dynamic landscape of thoughts, memories, and beliefs, plays a crucial role in how one experiences liberation and rebirth. Practitioners are guided to approach each session with openness, a willingness to observe without judgment, and an acceptance of whatever emerges. Letting go of rigid expectations is key; in these moments, the mind steps back, allowing deeper layers of awareness to surface. The participant's role becomes that of a gentle observer, creating an inner space where self-discovery can unfold organically, free from mental resistance or interference.

An equally essential aspect of preparation lies within the environment itself. Every element, from the lighting to the scent of the air, contributes to the overall experience, shaping the emotional and mental states that arise. The space should be a sanctuary, imbued with calm and protected from external distractions. Dim lighting or candlelight can encourage a sense of warmth and safety, allowing the participant to settle into a state of receptivity. Elements like soothing aromas, soft textures, or natural sounds ground the participant, anchoring them in the present moment and cultivating a profound sense of connection to the space.

Setting clear intentions, though simple in nature, holds the power to shape the entire experience. An intention acts as a compass, a guiding light that directs one's focus and energy throughout the therapeutic journey. Before beginning, practitioners are encouraged to reflect on their purpose—whether it's to release old emotions, find clarity, or deepen self-understanding. With a clear intention, each breath, each feeling, and each movement aligns with this purpose, making the process a powerful exercise in mindful transformation.

Within liberation therapy, the concept of boundaries is not overlooked. Participants are reminded of their autonomy throughout the process; they are the keepers of their own experience, free to pause, adjust, or redirect their focus as needed. This respect for personal boundaries is vital, creating a foundation of trust and self-care that enhances the therapeutic potential. Through this self-awareness, participants come to recognize their own limits and can explore their inner world without fear, knowing they are in control at every stage of the journey.

Preparation, then, is an invitation to enter this space with reverence, with a respect for the mind, body, and spirit. It is a grounding ritual, a way of honoring oneself before taking the first step into unknown realms of consciousness. With each element prepared, the participant stands at the threshold, ready to surrender to the therapeutic process. This preparation marks the beginning of a sacred journey, where the familiar self is left behind, and the potential for rebirth emerges on the horizon.

As the preparatory stage deepens, attention turns to the inner environment, an unseen landscape where emotions, thoughts, and energies converge to create a fertile ground for transformation. Effective preparation for liberation and rebirth extends beyond physical readiness; it requires an alignment of mind, spirit, and the space that holds the ritual. In these moments of reflection and intention-setting, one creates an inner sanctuary, a mental and emotional setting that welcomes profound change with openness and courage.

Central to this phase is the intentional design of the therapeutic space. Practitioners are encouraged to craft an environment that holds not only physical safety but also a sense of emotional and energetic security. The selection of symbols and objects can influence this setting—items like crystals, plants, or small tokens of personal significance that reflect protection, healing, or guidance. Each chosen object, each carefully placed item, imbues the space with purpose, resonating with the participant's goals and intentions. Here, the external and internal worlds merge; the environment becomes a reflection of the participant's journey, a sacred space where transformation can flourish.

Equally vital is the role of breath in preparing the mind and body for this journey. Breath, the life force that animates all experience, is a bridge between the conscious and subconscious, a pathway to the depths of one's own spirit. Simple breathing exercises such as deep, slow inhalations or rhythmic patterns help calm the mind, slow the heart rate, and bring focus to the present moment. Through these gentle practices, participants begin to feel the connection between their physical and energetic bodies, sensing subtle currents that flow within. As the breath steadies, the mind follows, attuning itself to the natural rhythm of the body and creating space for the exploration that lies ahead.

Mental clarity is the foundation upon which the liberation and rebirth process is built. Before beginning, participants are encouraged to engage in brief mindfulness exercises, emptying the mind of excess thoughts and focusing entirely on the sensation of presence. Visualization techniques can be especially powerful here, guiding the mind to release scattered energies and draw inward, like a retreat into the depths of one's own consciousness. Visualizing a protective, calming light enveloping the body or imagining oneself grounded by strong, anchoring roots invites peace and focus, a state that enhances the ability to move deeply into the therapeutic work without distraction or interference.

Emotional preparation is no less significant. The inner landscape can be a labyrinth of hidden fears, aspirations, and memories, and this phase encourages participants to meet each feeling with acceptance. Allowing emotions to flow freely, unbound by judgment, is essential for liberation; one must embrace the complexity of their emotional self, acknowledging both light and shadow without inhibition. As participants open to these feelings, they initiate a subtle release, softening the walls around repressed emotions and making way for the profound release that is integral to rebirth.

As practitioners continue this preparation, they are guided to cultivate a sense of trust—both in themselves and in the process that will unfold. This trust allows for a willingness to let go, a sense of security in the unknown that supports the entirety of the liberation journey. Within this trusting state, participants create a mental environment that mirrors their physical setting: a space that is stable, protected, and open to whatever arises. Each breath, each intention, and each feeling becomes a participant in this delicate dance of self-discovery and release.

At the heart of these preparations lies a sacred act of acknowledgment—a recognition of the journey ahead and the courage it requires. This stage of preparation is a conscious step toward embracing the unknown, a willingness to confront the layers of self with honesty and compassion. It is a passage, a deepening of commitment to the therapeutic path that will soon lead to a place where the self, stripped of its past limitations, can emerge transformed and renewed. Here, within the safe bounds of mind, body, and spirit, the groundwork for liberation and rebirth is complete, and the journey inward begins in earnest.

Chapter 3
Meditation and Breathing Techniques

Breath is the silent guide in the journey of liberation and rebirth, a thread that connects the conscious mind to deeper realms of experience. Meditation and breathing techniques lay the foundation for this journey, acting as both compass and anchor. Through focused breathing and quiet meditation, one steps into a heightened awareness, moving closer to the quiet spaces within where true liberation begins. Each breath becomes a ritual, a movement of energy that reveals hidden layers of the self and brings clarity to the surface.

In the earliest stages of meditation, participants are guided to focus on the natural rhythm of their breath, following each inhale and exhale without effort or alteration. This simple act initiates a state of mindfulness, a space where distractions fade and one's awareness sharpens. The breath serves as a portal, leading the mind into stillness, and within this stillness, thoughts lose their power to disrupt. The breath becomes a soothing presence, an unwavering companion through the initial steps of rebirth, inviting the participant to turn inward, to listen to what lies beneath the noise of everyday life.

With attention fixed upon the breath, deeper patterns in the body and mind begin to emerge. Breathing practices within liberation therapy are not arbitrary; each technique is designed to unveil hidden emotions, thoughts, or energetic knots that may have lingered unnoticed. For instance, diaphragmatic breathing—a practice of drawing air deeply into the abdomen rather than the chest—enables a more expansive release, connecting to the body's core where many emotions are stored. As the diaphragm moves with each breath, it sends waves of calm throughout the body, loosening tension in areas that often hold stress, such as the neck, shoulders, and lower back.

Another essential technique is counted breathing, a practice of inhaling, holding, and exhaling according to a slow, rhythmic count. This pattern of breathing not only calms the nervous system but also encourages the mind to settle into a focused, meditative state. Each count guides the participant further from external concerns and brings them closer to the inner space where healing can begin. The deliberate rhythm becomes a mantra, a steady cadence that encourages the heart rate to slow and thoughts to dissolve, creating an ideal state for introspection and release.

Visualization techniques are often paired with these breathing practices, enhancing the meditative experience and allowing participants to engage with their inner world on a more symbolic level. Participants may be invited to envision each inhale as a stream of cleansing light, filling the body with warmth, and each exhale as a release of stagnant energy or tension. This visualization deepens the sensation of release, providing a visual language to the experience of liberation. Through this practice, breath transforms into a tool of transformation, not merely oxygenating the body but also unbinding emotional and energetic residues that no longer serve.

As the participant moves through these exercises, the breath begins to unlock deeper layers of awareness. It stirs emotions, awakens memories, and brings subtle energies to the surface—elements often buried within the unconscious mind. Each breath holds the potential for revelation, a spark that illuminates past experiences or forgotten fragments of the self. This gentle unfolding allows the participant to witness their inner world with compassion, observing emotions as they arise without the need to control or suppress them. Here, the breath becomes a mirror, reflecting the hidden aspects of the self and inviting a release from old patterns.

By cultivating a practice of focused breathing and meditation, participants establish an intimate connection with their own life force, the energy that sustains both body and spirit. They become conscious of the power that lies in each breath, recognizing that liberation is not found in grand gestures but in the quiet, consistent act of returning to oneself. Through this practice, they step closer to a state of rebirth, where each breath signifies a letting go and each moment holds the possibility of renewal. The simple act of breathing transforms into a sacred rhythm, a dance between release and reception, guiding the participant toward the heart of their own liberation.

As the exploration of meditation and breathing deepens, participants are introduced to advanced techniques that tap into the profound energetic currents within. Breath, once gentle and rhythmic, now becomes an instrument of awakening, moving energy through subtle pathways and unlocking areas long held in shadow. With each practice, participants are guided further into the realms of the self, where layers of identity dissolve, and the spirit breathes freely. Here, breathing transcends the physical; it becomes an alchemical process that unites body, mind, and spirit, preparing the practitioner for the liberating depths of rebirth.

A key technique in this phase is circular breathing, a continuous form of breath without pause between inhale and exhale, which cultivates a state of flow, releasing tension and resistance. Through this uninterrupted cycle, the participant encounters a heightened awareness, entering a trance-like state that eases the mind's grip on reality. This practice, used in traditions such as shamanic rituals and deep meditative disciplines, creates a bridge to the subconscious, allowing hidden thoughts, images, and energies to surface. With each unbroken breath, there is a dissolution of boundaries, as though the participant steps beyond the conscious mind into a broader, more expansive field of awareness.

To accompany circular breathing, techniques like alternate nostril breathing (known in yogic traditions as nadi shodhana) are also introduced. This technique balances the left and right hemispheres of the brain, aligning logical thought with intuitive insight. By alternating breaths between nostrils, participants engage the body's energy channels, or nadis, which are believed to direct the life force throughout the body. This balancing act not only clears mental fog but also promotes a harmonious flow of energy, creating a calm yet alert state that enhances the experience of self-discovery. In liberation therapy, this balance is essential, ensuring that practitioners remain grounded even as they journey through profound emotional and energetic landscapes.

As these advanced techniques begin to reveal underlying emotional currents, the breath takes on the role of a silent guide, bringing attention to areas of resistance or emotional intensity. Participants may encounter memories or emotions they had buried, sensations that rise and fall with each breath. To support this, practices such as intentional breath holds are introduced. Holding the breath at the peak of an inhale or the depth of an exhale creates moments of intensity, a pause that invites the body and mind to process and release long-held energies. The breath hold becomes a moment of surrender, a space where stored emotions soften, loosen, and drift into awareness, allowing for a quiet release.

Another profound practice within this phase is energy visualization, where participants are encouraged to envision each breath as a vibrant current of light or energy. As they inhale, they visualize this energy gathering at points of tension or discomfort within the body; as they exhale, they imagine it dispersing, taking with it any sense of unease or emotional weight. This visualization infuses the breathing practice with intention, creating a vivid sense of cleansing and renewal. Each breath becomes a purifying act, drawing in life and expelling what no longer serves, preparing the participant for the deeper transformations that lie ahead.

Through these techniques, participants learn that breath is more than a simple function—it is a gateway to the soul's inner workings, a rhythm that mirrors the cycles of life, death, and rebirth within oneself. As they advance in their practice, they come to recognize how each technique allows them to access deeper states of consciousness, peeling away the layers that often mask their true nature. Breath becomes the vehicle of self-liberation, a path that enables them to release repressed energies and engage with parts of themselves that were once hidden.

This phase of breathing and meditation is not just a preparatory exercise; it is a rite of passage. Each inhale, each exhale, brings the participant closer to the raw essence of self, to the core from which liberation springs. With every session, breath guides them to that quiet place of rebirth, where past limitations dissolve and new possibilities emerge. Here, in the quiet stillness of focused breathwork, participants prepare to cross the threshold into a world unbound by past burdens, liberated by the rhythm of their own breath.

Chapter 4
Identifying and Releasing Emotional Blockages

Within the path of liberation and rebirth therapy, the recognition and release of emotional blockages stands as one of the most transformative steps. These blockages—energetic knots formed through unprocessed emotions, past traumas, and deeply rooted beliefs—often govern our thoughts, behaviors, and reactions, exerting a silent influence on the course of our lives. They are imprints left by experiences long buried, yet they shape how we see ourselves and interact with the world. By bringing awareness to these blockages, one can unravel the restrictive threads that bind the spirit, allowing for a flow of renewed energy and clarity of purpose.

Self-observation is the first step in identifying these subtle barriers. Through mindful reflection, one can cultivate the awareness needed to recognize patterns that indicate emotional blockages. Participants are encouraged to notice recurring thoughts, habits, or intense emotional responses that arise in specific situations. Perhaps anger flares unexpectedly, or a deep sadness lingers without an apparent cause; these reactions are often signs of hidden energies that await acknowledgment. Self-observation, in this context, is not simply introspection; it is an intentional, compassionate witnessing of one's inner landscape, free from judgment or the need to fix or alter.

As awareness deepens, participants may begin to trace these responses to their origins. Memories surface, and images or sensations accompany them—hints of past events that left their mark. Through this journey into memory, one can begin to understand the energetic weight carried within. The body, too, speaks of these blockages, as it holds emotional memories within muscles, joints, and organs. Tension in the chest, stiffness in the neck, or knots in the stomach may serve as physical manifestations of repressed emotions, silently signaling the presence of unhealed wounds.

Breath becomes an invaluable ally in uncovering these blockages. Deep, intentional breathing guides awareness through the body, revealing areas where energy feels dense or stagnant. Practitioners may place a hand over these regions, breathing into them as though to loosen and dissolve the hidden layers. With each breath, the mind descends deeper into the body's sensations, and as tensions release, insights and emotions begin to arise. This process requires patience and gentleness; blockages built over years often reveal themselves slowly, allowing the practitioner to approach their inner landscape without force or urgency.

Visualization techniques further aid in identifying emotional barriers. Participants might imagine their body as a vast, luminous field, scanning from head to toe and visualizing any darkened or tense areas as places where blockages reside. These visualized areas can then be softened, illuminated by an inner light, as though each breath infuses them with warmth and openness. The act of seeing these areas, even within the mind's eye, often reveals hidden messages—memories, sensations, or emotions tied to specific experiences. This visualization process creates a safe, contained space where one can connect with emotions that might otherwise be challenging to access.

Introspection is not merely a mental exercise; it requires the courage to fully experience the emotions as they emerge. In liberation therapy, releasing blockages entails a willingness to feel—to allow sadness, anger, or grief to flow freely without repression or control. Tears may surface, tremors may ripple through the body, and breath may become deeper and more intense. These are signs of release, movements of energy as it shifts from the inner to the outer world. Through this emotional flow, the body purges itself of these remnants, creating space for new and lighter energies to take root.

As one connects more deeply with these sensations, there is a growing realization that these blockages are neither obstacles nor faults but teachers on the path of self-understanding. Each blockage holds a story, a memory, a lesson waiting to be heard. By approaching these emotions with openness and curiosity, participants come to see them as parts of the journey rather than barriers to it. This acceptance is essential, for it transforms the healing process into an act of compassion—a reunion with the fragmented aspects of the self that were once cast aside.

Through this practice, participants initiate a gentle release, not through force but through acceptance. Emotional unblocking becomes a dance between awareness and release, a rhythmic process that allows the spirit to shed the layers that once weighed it down. Here, in the quiet surrender of the moment, the first waves of liberation begin, setting the soul on its path to a profound rebirth.

As the journey into emotional unblocking continues, deeper techniques emerge, revealing methods that facilitate the release of emotions embedded within one's energetic and physical being. Having identified the presence of emotional blockages, practitioners now turn to practices that invite these energies to shift, dissolve, and ultimately, depart. This process of release is a healing ritual, a gentle unbinding that calls upon awareness, breath, and body-centered techniques to release energetic residues and welcome emotional freedom.

One of the foundational practices for release is known as active breathwork, a powerful form of breath that intensifies the clearing of emotional blockages. In this technique, participants practice rapid and rhythmic breathing, consciously drawing breath into the core of any physical or emotional discomfort. The breath acts like a wave, dislodging emotional and energetic patterns that may have calcified over time. With each exhalation, a release occurs, as though layers of memory, tension, and emotion are lifted and released with the flow of air. Breathwork in this context becomes more than a technique; it is a sacred rhythm, one that transforms breath into a vehicle of liberation.

Alongside breathwork, somatic exercises provide another pathway for emotional release. Somatic practices emphasize the physical expressions of emotions—those subtle tensions, contractions, or postures that embody what has long been held within. Participants are encouraged to tune into these physical sensations and allow movement to flow intuitively. Perhaps the body sways, trembles, or stretches in response to an emotion; these movements are seen not as random, but as essential acts of liberation. This process honors the body's innate wisdom, giving it permission to express and release what words cannot, allowing energy to move and emotions to unfurl naturally.

Sound, too, becomes a tool for release. The vibrations created by vocalizing, whether through hums, chants, or simple sounds, resonate deeply within the body, loosening areas that feel dense or blocked. The practice of toning, for instance, involves releasing sustained vocal tones, focusing sound into specific areas of tension or emotional heaviness. This act of sounding resonates on multiple levels, grounding participants in their physical form while also creating an energetic pathway for release. The voice, freed from inhibition, becomes a bridge between inner experiences and external expression, a soundscape for energies that have long remained silent.

Visualization practices can be woven into these techniques, offering participants a symbolic representation of their release. Guided by an inner vision, one might imagine energetic blockages as dark clouds or tangled roots that dissipate with each exhale or dissolve with each movement. In this visualization, emotions and memories take form, granting participants a clear image of what they are letting go. The visualized release not only aids the mind in understanding the process but also reinforces the energetic shift, as though seeing the release makes it more tangible, more real. As each imagined thread dissolves, a sense of lightness fills the spaces once occupied by these energetic remnants.

Journaling and reflective writing complement these practices by allowing participants to articulate the subtleties of their experience. After engaging in breathwork, sound, or movement, writing provides a structured space for reflection and integration. Emotions, memories, and insights that emerged during the release can be translated into words, capturing the essence of what has been released and what lingers. This written record becomes a witness to one's journey, an acknowledgment of the courage it takes to confront, feel, and release old burdens.

In group settings, the act of sharing these experiences with others adds yet another dimension to the release process. When participants feel safe to share their insights and emotions, a collective energy arises, as though each individual's journey is mirrored in the experiences of others. This shared vulnerability breaks down barriers, creating a supportive environment that amplifies the impact of each person's release. In such settings, collective breathwork, shared toning, or group meditation can further enhance the unblocking process, infusing the space with a profound energy that transcends individual limitations.

Releasing blockages requires trust in the process and a willingness to surrender to emotions as they arise. The deeper one travels, the more layers begin to unfurl, each release revealing another aspect of self, hidden behind years of conditioning and self-protection. This journey to unblocking is neither a single event nor a linear path; it is an unfolding, a series of experiences that peel away the layers of past experiences, unveiling a new sense of freedom and emotional clarity. Each session becomes a step forward, a moment where breath, movement, and intention converge to reveal and release what no longer serves.

Through these practices, participants move closer to liberation, shedding layers of fear, grief, and resistance to reach a place of emotional openness. With each session, the weight of past experiences lightens, and the self becomes more present, more expansive. In this space of release, liberation takes on a tangible form—the beginning of a rebirth that redefines the self, freed from the constraints of old blockages, ready to embrace the fullness of the journey ahead.

Chapter 5
Fundamental Liberation Practices

Liberation rituals are the heartbeats of this journey, ancient practices that serve as gateways to the soul's profound release and renewal. Within these rituals, participants encounter the opportunity to liberate themselves from the patterns, memories, and emotions that have accumulated over lifetimes. Each ritual is both personal and universal—a space where the soul recognizes its boundless nature, unburdened by the weight of the past. Here, we begin to explore the foundational practices that guide individuals through the transformative process of liberation, creating intentional moments where spirit, breath, and intention converge to usher in freedom.

One of the most elemental practices in liberation therapy is the ritual of release. This ritual is crafted around the act of consciously letting go. Participants gather symbols, objects, or written notes that represent memories, emotions, or habits they are ready to release. These tokens, imbued with the weight of past experiences, are honored as teachers on the journey thus far. In the ritual, participants choose a method for releasing these symbols—perhaps burning, burying, or setting them adrift in water. The chosen method creates a tangible manifestation of release, transforming the invisible into something felt, seen, and experienced, leaving the participant with a sense of renewed lightness.

In addition to physical rituals, there is the practice of intention-setting, a cornerstone of liberation work. Intentions act as compasses, guiding participants toward the aspects of self that require healing, insight, or release. In this practice, participants sit quietly, focusing inward, and allow the desired intention to arise naturally—whether it is the release of fear, the invitation of courage, or the acceptance of self. As this intention is set, it becomes an energetic beacon, a quiet force that aligns each step of the ritual with purpose. With this guiding intention, the ritual's potency deepens, drawing in energies that resonate with the participant's personal journey.

Another essential practice is energy purification, a process of cleansing both the physical and energetic fields that surround each individual. This ritual often involves the use of elements, each chosen for its unique qualities and its symbolic power. Smudging with sacred herbs, for example, invites the element of air to carry away stagnant energies, while water rituals cleanse the emotional body, allowing old pains to wash away. Fire ceremonies, where participants release written memories into flames, symbolize transformation and rebirth. Each element plays its role, creating a purified space within and around the participant, enhancing their ability to release without resistance.

Grounding practices are also woven into liberation rituals, anchoring the participant to the earth and the present moment. These practices often involve physical contact with the earth—standing barefoot, placing hands on soil, or visualizing roots extending deep into the ground. Grounding acts as a stabilizing force, ensuring that as the participant releases old energies, they remain steady and balanced, connected to the world around them. This rootedness provides the foundation needed to move through challenging emotions, offering a sense of protection as participants journey through the depths of their own psyche.

A central practice within liberation rituals is the guided visualization journey, where participants are led through an inner landscape to confront, understand, and release energies or memories. In these visualizations, they may journey to symbolic places—a serene forest, a peaceful river, or a glowing temple—each space chosen to facilitate release. Within these imagined realms, participants encounter aspects of themselves, witnessing old memories or emotions with compassion and understanding. In this safe inner space, they are encouraged to let go, visualizing emotions dissipating like mist or being absorbed by the earth. The symbolic nature of these visualizations allows participants to engage deeply with their inner world, facing and releasing energies in a way that feels safe, yet profound.

The power of sound also finds its place within liberation rituals, often through drumming, chanting, or toning. The resonance created by sound travels through the body, loosening tight emotions and stirring energies that may have long remained dormant. Participants might engage in rhythmic drumming or chanting, feeling vibrations resonate through their being. Sound, in these moments, becomes a vehicle for release, carrying emotions, memories, and energies outward, freeing the body and spirit to move more fluidly through the experience of rebirth.

Within these foundational liberation practices, there lies a balance between ritual and spontaneity. Each participant is encouraged to create a practice that feels true to their inner needs, adapting elements as guided by intuition. The ritual space thus becomes a sacred, adaptable arena where each individual can express, release, and ultimately, transform in a way that aligns with their unique journey.

Through these liberation practices, participants begin to reclaim their inherent freedom, unburdened by past influences that once shaped their lives. Each ritual, whether rooted in silence, movement, or symbolic action, moves them closer to an essential truth: liberation is not a destination but a continuous unfolding, a peeling away of what is no longer needed, revealing the luminous essence of the self. In these moments, the spirit glimpses its own boundless nature, standing at the threshold of a profound rebirth.

Building upon the core practices of liberation, participants move into the details of ritual variation and adaptation, tailoring each practice to meet their evolving needs. The depth of each ritual experience is shaped by the participant's intention, readiness, and personal growth, and as such, liberation rituals are dynamic—changing and expanding in harmony with the individual's journey. Here, practical guidance and nuanced adaptations bring a deeper understanding to each ritual, helping participants access layers of self previously untouched, as they transform release into a deliberate and empowering process.

One of the most adaptable aspects of liberation rituals is the method of symbolic release. While burning or burying objects tied to past emotions is a common practice, variations allow participants to personalize this act. For instance, participants may find resonance in working with water, releasing petals or stones into a river or sea, symbolizing the release of attachments to be carried away by the natural current. This can be especially powerful for those seeking a gentler form of release, as water represents emotion and fluidity, encouraging a gradual surrender. Each chosen method allows for unique expression and ensures that the ritual feels connected to one's true intentions, rather than following a rigid form.

In more advanced stages of ritual work, participants are encouraged to incorporate personal totems or symbols of strength that serve as reminders of their resilience. These symbols, such as a feather, stone, or handwritten phrase, are kept close during the ritual and represent the inner resources that the participant calls upon when confronting challenging emotions. After each session, these symbols may be placed in a sacred space or altar, creating a tangible connection to the strength cultivated in the ritual. This practice helps participants ground their liberation journey in the physical world, making their progress and resilience visible in daily life.

Additional techniques such as fasting or silence can also enhance the potency of liberation rituals, especially when the participant seeks to amplify focus and introspection. Fasting before a ritual, even if brief, brings heightened awareness, as the body's energy is directed inward rather than toward digestion. This practice is ancient, present in spiritual traditions around the world, and serves to bring clarity to the mind while reducing distractions. Silence, too, holds powerful energy; refraining from speech for a set period prior to the ritual allows the participant to internalize their experience and foster a sense of sacredness, a quiet anticipation that sets the stage for the release work ahead.

Group settings introduce another dimension to liberation practices, providing the support and energy of a shared experience. In group rituals, participants may engage in synchronized breathwork, chanting, or drumming, generating a collective rhythm that amplifies the energy of each individual's release. Each participant, though focused on their own liberation, becomes part of a communal energy flow, where the shared intention to release creates a synergy of healing. This environment fosters a unique connection, as participants witness each other's courage and vulnerability, reinforcing the sense of being seen, supported, and honored in one's journey.

Sound-based techniques also deepen in this phase, where participants experiment with chanting and mantras, each sound designed to resonate with specific chakras or energy centers. For example, sounds such as "OM" or "AH" are known to vibrate through the heart and crown chakras, opening pathways for deeper emotional and spiritual release. Participants are encouraged to experiment, finding which sounds resonate most powerfully within their bodies, and to engage in vocal toning as a release mechanism. These sounds stir the emotions and energies that have become stagnant, loosening their hold and creating space for new energetic flow.

Visualization, likewise, can be tailored to the participant's unique inner world. While some may visualize light enveloping areas of tension, others may find power in imagining roots extending from their body into the earth, carrying away stagnant energies. These visualizations can shift based on intention—for instance, one might envision their heart as a radiant sphere, expanding with each breath, or imagine past memories as leaves, falling and dissolving into the ground. In these moments, visualization becomes a deeply personal dialogue between the conscious mind and the subconscious, where each symbol holds meaning that resonates uniquely within the participant.

Advanced practices of gratitude and reflection are woven into the end of each ritual, creating a conscious closure to the process. Here, participants are encouraged to acknowledge the emotions and energies they have released, giving thanks to these parts of themselves for the roles they played, even if painful or burdensome. This expression of gratitude is not only a gesture of closure but also a way of honoring the journey itself, recognizing that each released emotion or memory once served a purpose. This practice of gratitude reinforces compassion, as the participant moves forward without resentment or lingering attachments to the past, with an open heart and an awareness of the growth that has emerged from these experiences.

By understanding and personalizing these liberation practices, participants cultivate a ritual that resonates deeply with their evolving selves. Each method, adapted and refined, creates a powerful space where release becomes an act of self-empowerment rather than a simple letting go. The rituals take on a rhythm, a flow that is unique to each individual, allowing them to journey through the layers of self with curiosity, compassion, and strength. In these practices, liberation is experienced as an ongoing process—a dance between release and renewal, where the soul continuously sheds what no longer serves, stepping ever closer to a state of wholeness and rebirth.

Chapter 6
Connection with the Inner Self

The journey toward liberation and rebirth leads one inevitably inward, to the quiet depths where the true self resides. This connection with the inner self is a sacred exploration, a movement beyond surface identities and external labels, into the core of one's own essence. Here, in this place untouched by life's noise, lies the pure consciousness that shapes perception, meaning, and purpose. Developing this connection is not only fundamental to the liberation process; it is the anchor that allows one to experience each ritual, each release, as a return to wholeness.

To begin this inner exploration, participants are encouraged to create a space of stillness, a silent sanctuary within. In this stillness, free from external distractions, one can cultivate the gentle practice of self-observation. This is not merely watching thoughts as they arise; it is a state of conscious witnessing, a way of perceiving without judgment or attachment. By observing the mind as it naturally ebbs and flows, participants begin to understand the subtle workings of their own consciousness. They notice recurring themes, emotions, and thoughts—each revealing aspects of the self that had once been hidden.

As this self-observation deepens, meditation becomes a powerful tool to anchor one's awareness in the present moment. Focusing on the breath, one feels the rhythm of life moving through the body, connecting the conscious mind to the deeper currents of inner awareness. Through this practice, participants find themselves descending gently into the layers of the mind, beyond daily worries and identities. This meditative state becomes a gateway, a place where one begins to feel the essence of the inner self—calm, timeless, and boundless, untouched by external concerns or conditioning.

Guided visualization offers another path to connect with the inner self. In these visualizations, participants might imagine themselves standing at the edge of a vast, serene landscape—perhaps a forest, an ocean, or a mountain. Each participant chooses a scene that resonates deeply with their spirit, a place that feels like home. Here, within this imagined realm, they meet the quiet and wise presence of their inner self, perhaps visualized as a light, an energy, or a guide. Through this interaction, a profound sense of familiarity emerges, as though reconnecting with a part of the self that has always been present but rarely acknowledged.

The practice of journaling serves to bridge this connection further. After meditation or visualization, participants are encouraged to write freely, capturing any thoughts, images, or feelings that surfaced. These entries, written without censorship or judgment, reveal subtle insights about the self, reflections that often remain hidden in the flow of daily life. The act of writing deepens awareness, grounding the experiences of meditation and visualization into tangible form. As participants revisit these entries, they recognize patterns, desires, and deeper truths, each journal entry a step closer to understanding the nature of their inner self.

Connecting with the inner self also requires embracing the duality within. Each individual holds both light and shadow, aspects of the self that reflect beauty and strength as well as fear and limitation. Liberation is found not in denying the shadow, but in facing it with compassion and curiosity. By acknowledging these darker aspects, participants come to understand that they are not defined by their fears or regrets, but rather, by their ability to observe and embrace these facets. In doing so, they reclaim their wholeness, recognizing that each part of the self has value and a purpose in the greater journey of self-discovery.

Breathwork, too, remains a steadfast guide. When emotions arise, the breath serves as an anchor, a steady presence that grounds the individual in the experience without becoming lost within it. Each inhale and exhale brings clarity, allowing participants to move deeper into the layers of their inner self, breathing through emotions, memories, and realizations. The breath becomes a reminder of their autonomy and resilience, a constant rhythm that supports their journey into the unknown territories of the soul.

In this process, participants learn to listen to the quiet messages of their own spirit. This is a different kind of listening—one that requires patience, openness, and trust in the unfolding of each moment. As they quiet the mind, they begin to perceive the subtle whispers of intuition, the gentle nudges that guide them toward their truth. This inner voice, often overlooked, becomes a source of wisdom and strength, a guiding presence that aligns the outer self with the deeper needs and desires of the soul.

As participants cultivate this connection with the inner self, a profound shift occurs. They no longer seek validation or meaning from external sources; instead, they find a steady and unwavering sense of self within. Each ritual, each breath, and each release brings them closer to this center, this essence that remains constant amid change. Here, in the sacred space of the inner self, participants experience a liberation that is both profound and enduring—a freedom that arises from the simple, yet transformative act of knowing oneself deeply, without hesitation or fear. Through this journey, they stand not only in liberation but in the quiet power of their true, boundless nature.

As the journey of connecting with the inner self deepens, practices become more refined, guiding participants toward a profound intimacy with their own consciousness. This stage is not simply about self-observation but about merging with the quiet, unchanging awareness that lies beyond thoughts, emotions, and memories. Each technique becomes a doorway into the subtle realms, an invitation to transcend the surface layers and encounter the essence of self that exists independent of external influences.

Through these practices, participants cultivate a heightened sensitivity to the messages that emerge within, gaining insights that reveal the deeper wisdom of their soul.

One of the most transformative tools for deepening this connection is the practice of self-inquiry. Through self-inquiry, participants ask simple yet powerful questions, such as "Who am I beyond my roles, beliefs, and experiences?" This question is not meant to be answered logically but to be explored through direct experience. With each breath and moment of silence, participants are encouraged to feel into the question, allowing layers of identity to dissolve. In this state, they may experience brief moments where the mind becomes quiet, and the sense of self expands beyond personal history. Here, in these spaces of pure awareness, the essence of the inner self begins to reveal itself, unbounded and expansive.

Guided meditation provides another path to enter these deeper layers, using imagery that evokes the timeless qualities of the self. In this advanced stage, participants might visualize themselves as light or energy, observing how this energy flows beyond the physical form and merges with the environment around them. This visualization dissolves the barriers between the self and the world, blurring the boundaries that create separation. As they immerse in this sensation, participants may feel a profound sense of unity—a recognition that the essence of self is interconnected with the greater fabric of existence, a connection that transcends individuality and expands into the universal.

A powerful practice for reinforcing this inner connection is self-compassion meditation, where participants focus on sending kindness, acceptance, and love to all parts of themselves, especially those aspects they may have struggled with. By visualizing the inner self as a loving presence, they allow compassion to flow through their thoughts and emotions, embracing every layer with understanding. This practice transforms self-criticism into self-acceptance, softening the inner barriers that prevent connection with the true self. Each session strengthens the bond with the inner self, teaching participants that liberation comes not from rejecting any part of themselves but from integrating all aspects with compassion.

Silence itself becomes a powerful tool in these practices. Spending extended time in silence allows participants to disengage from the constant flow of thoughts, fostering a state of deep reflection. When freed from external noise, the mind naturally turns inward, revealing insights that often lie beneath the surface. Silence offers the space to hear the inner voice clearly, to feel the subtle shifts of energy, and to observe the natural rhythm of the self. Participants may begin to feel that silence is not the absence of sound, but the presence of a deeper, more profound form of communication—an intimate language of the soul that speaks without words.

The use of affirmations that resonate with one's deepest truths also serves to strengthen the inner connection. Participants are encouraged to create simple, heartfelt affirmations such as "I am whole," "I trust in my inner wisdom," or "I am free from fear." Repeating these affirmations during meditation or at the beginning of each day gradually rewires the subconscious, allowing these truths to take root. Over time, these affirmations become living reminders of the inner self's boundless potential and purity, subtly shifting perceptions and opening pathways to deeper self-trust and authenticity.

Journaling continues to be a valuable tool, especially for capturing insights and intuitions that arise from meditation and self-inquiry. Participants are encouraged to record their experiences in detail, noting any sensations, emotions, or visions that emerge. In this stage, the journal becomes a mirror, reflecting the unfolding relationship with the inner self. By revisiting entries over time, participants can observe the shifts within their consciousness, patterns in their insights, and areas of growth. This practice provides a tangible way to witness the evolution of the self, grounding the often intangible experiences of inner connection in written form.

Another practice that aids in accessing the wisdom of the inner self is dream journaling, where participants record dreams upon waking. Dreams, in their symbolic language, reveal truths about the unconscious mind, often shedding light on aspects of the self that are hidden during waking life. By capturing and reflecting on these dreams, participants gain insight into the desires, fears, and intuitions that guide their inner journey. With regular practice, dream journaling becomes a dialogue with the subconscious, allowing for an ongoing exploration of the self in the ethereal realms of sleep, where the inner voice speaks in symbols and imagery.

The final layer of this connection is found in surrender—a willingness to release control, trust the process, and allow the inner self to guide. Surrender is not passive; it is a conscious choice to accept the unfolding of each moment without resistance. In surrender, participants release the need to define or control the outcome of their journey, embracing instead the mysterious and organic nature of self-discovery. This surrender brings a profound peace, a sense that they are held by something greater, something vast yet deeply intimate. The inner self, no longer constrained by fear or expectation, rises to reveal its wisdom, guiding each step with grace.

Through these practices, participants cultivate an enduring, sacred connection with the inner self—a presence that remains steady and whole, even in the midst of life's changes. This bond brings clarity, resilience, and profound peace, empowering individuals to live from a place of truth. As they continue to journey within, they come to understand that liberation is not found in changing or escaping the self, but in embracing its full, infinite nature. In this space of inner unity, they experience a true rebirth, not as a new person, but as a more authentic, deeply connected version of themselves.

Chapter 7
Trauma and Energetic Imprints

Traumas, whether recent or distant, shape the energetic and emotional body, creating imprints that influence thoughts, emotions, and even physical health. These energetic imprints are echoes of past experiences that linger within, often silently guiding responses, fears, and beliefs. In the process of liberation and rebirth therapy, understanding and identifying these imprints is an essential step, allowing one to explore how past traumas have affected the mind, body, and spirit and to begin the journey toward healing.

Each trauma, from seemingly minor events to significant life-altering moments, carries an energetic signature. The body and mind absorb these events deeply, embedding reactions, memories, and sensations that may reemerge unexpectedly, triggered by familiar sights, sounds, or situations. Participants are invited to reflect on memories or emotions that surface in their daily lives or during rituals—moments that elicit a reaction disproportionate to the present event often reveal a deeper, underlying imprint. By observing these reactions without judgment, participants start to trace these imprints to their origins, revealing the hidden influences of past experiences on their current state.

The energetic body, much like the physical body, has its pathways and centers that hold and distribute energy. Imprints from trauma can disrupt this natural flow, creating blockages or areas of excessive tension. For example, traumas connected to feelings of vulnerability or fear may manifest as tightness in the chest or shoulders, while suppressed anger can appear as tension in the jaw or hands. By learning to tune into the body's sensations, participants start to sense where energies are trapped, creating a roadmap to the places within that call for release and healing.

Through guided introspection, participants explore these sensations with gentle curiosity. Rather than attempting to avoid or suppress the discomfort, they are encouraged to breathe into the sensations, acknowledging each feeling as it arises. This process requires courage and patience, as each imprint often holds layers of emotions—grief, anger, fear, or sadness—that seek acknowledgment before they can be released. In this way, self-observation becomes a compassionate act, transforming discomfort into a gateway for understanding and healing the wounds within.

Journaling, once more, becomes a key tool in this exploration. Participants are encouraged to document the emotions and memories that surface, whether in meditation, during moments of heightened emotion, or even within the quiet spaces of everyday life. The act of writing transforms abstract feelings into words, giving shape to experiences that may have been difficult to articulate or even remember. Over time, these journal entries reveal patterns, connecting past events to current responses, and offering insights into how specific traumas have influenced one's life path and sense of self.

Visualization techniques further support the process of identifying and understanding these imprints. Participants might be guided to close their eyes and envision a symbolic representation of their trauma—a knot, a shadow, a locked door—within the body. This visualization serves as a bridge, making the invisible imprint visible and, thus, accessible. As participants observe the symbol with calm attention, they begin to interact with it, gently asking questions or simply witnessing it with acceptance. Through this act of witnessing, the imprint slowly begins to shift, opening the possibility for release.

For deeper introspection, breathwork once again becomes a central tool. Through specific breathing patterns, participants direct their breath to areas of tension or discomfort, gently encouraging these energetic knots to loosen. The breath carries life force into areas that may have felt numb or tense for years, infusing them with renewed awareness. With each inhale, the body invites in healing energy, and with each exhale, it releases fragments of the trapped emotions or memories that have long lingered within. Over time, this breathing practice transforms the relationship with past traumas, turning places of tension into spaces of peace and release.

In the journey of exploring trauma, participants come to understand that the aim is not to erase or negate these past experiences but to create space for them, allowing them to find a place within the broader narrative of their lives without disrupting the present. Traumas, in this context, become teachers—challenges that have shaped resilience, compassion, and strength. By shifting perspective, the participant begins to see the wisdom within these experiences, not defined by the suffering but by the profound growth that emerges from the process of healing.

Through these practices, participants gradually approach a place of peace, where the past no longer shadows the present. They come to understand that trauma, while impactful, does not define the whole of their being. In identifying and exploring these energetic imprints, they initiate the first steps toward liberation, creating a path that leads from recognition to healing, and ultimately, to the freedom and rebirth that lie on the other side.

As participants deepen their journey of exploring and releasing trauma, they step into the delicate process of consciously transforming the energetic imprints left by these experiences. The release of trauma is not simply about erasing pain but about integrating the lessons, emotions, and memories in a way that allows the self to find balance, acceptance, and empowerment. Here, techniques evolve to support a gentle yet profound healing, guiding participants through practices that facilitate both the release and integration of traumatic imprints, allowing them to move forward with renewed clarity and inner strength.

One of the fundamental practices in trauma release is somatic experiencing, a technique that brings focused awareness to the body's sensations as it processes and releases trauma. Participants are guided to tune into specific areas of tension or discomfort, observing how these sensations shift and change. This process requires patience, as each sensation may reveal layers of emotion or memory waiting to be acknowledged. By allowing the body to complete the physical response it could not fully express in the past—such as trembling, stretching, or releasing a long-held breath—the energetic residue of the trauma is gradually released, restoring the body's natural balance.

Guided imagery serves as a powerful complement to somatic experiencing, inviting participants to visualize their trauma as a symbolic image or object. This visualization might take the form of a heavy stone, a dark cloud, or even a locked door. Participants are then encouraged to interact with this image, visualizing it shrinking, dissolving, or transforming into something light and manageable. This act of transforming the image creates a sense of empowerment, allowing the participant to symbolically release and reshape the imprint. The visualized transformation becomes a ritual of release, an acknowledgment that they have the power to reshape their relationship with the trauma.

Breathwork remains a key technique, especially in the form of circular breathing—a continuous, rhythmic breathing pattern that helps release deep-seated emotions. Through circular breathing, participants cultivate a steady, uninterrupted flow of breath that bypasses mental resistance and directly reaches the emotional body. As the breath circulates, it loosens blockages, releasing fragments of memories or sensations that surface. With each exhale, participants allow these energies to dissipate, creating more space within the self. This practice can be both intense and liberating, as it encourages a deep surrender to the body's wisdom, allowing it to guide the healing process.

To support the release of trauma, participants may also engage in vocalization techniques, such as humming, chanting, or toning specific sounds. The vibrations generated by these sounds resonate through the body, breaking up energetic blockages and releasing emotions that words alone cannot express. Each sound, carefully chosen, targets specific areas or feelings within the body. For example, the deep hum of "OM" resonates through the chest, releasing tension around the heart, while the gentle chant of "AH" moves energy from the throat, encouraging expression. This vocal release can be subtle yet profoundly healing, as participants feel the vibrations reach and release places long held in silence.

Physical movement further amplifies the process, as participants are encouraged to follow the body's natural impulses to stretch, sway, or even dance. This intuitive movement allows the body to express and release energies that may feel restricted or stagnant. By tuning into how the body wishes to move, participants discover that healing is an active process, a dance between expression and release. Each movement becomes a ritual, a dialogue with the self that acknowledges and frees the emotions stored within muscles and tissues. In this embodied release, trauma is not fought or suppressed; it is transformed through movement, allowing the body to return to a state of fluidity and peace.

After each session of deep release, integration practices play a vital role. Journaling provides a structured space for reflection, allowing participants to capture the insights and emotions that surfaced. They are encouraged to write freely, noting any symbols, images, or thoughts that arose, and exploring how these elements connect to their overall healing journey. Journaling becomes a form of dialogue with the self, a way of witnessing and honoring the release that has occurred. These written reflections help anchor the experience, transforming it from an abstract sensation into a lived insight, a valuable part of the healing process.

A further integration practice involves creating a sacred ritual of closure, where participants consciously bring a sense of completion to each healing session. This ritual might include lighting a candle, offering gratitude, or placing a hand over the heart as a gesture of acknowledgment. Participants may take a few quiet moments to honor the courage it took to confront and release these imprints, recognizing that each act of release is an act of self-compassion and strength. This ritual becomes a symbolic ending, allowing participants to transition back into their daily lives with a renewed sense of grounding and balance.

Finally, grounding exercises ensure that participants feel rooted in the present, creating stability as they navigate the changes brought about by trauma release. Techniques such as placing the feet firmly on the earth, visualizing roots extending deep into the ground, or focusing on the steady rhythm of their own breath provide a sense of safety and support. Grounding reinforces the understanding that while the trauma is part of their story, it does not define them. With each grounding practice, participants return to the present moment, feeling strengthened and whole.

In this journey of release and integration, participants begin to see trauma not as an unchangeable wound but as a source of transformation. By engaging fully with these practices, they come to experience a profound liberation—the freedom to carry the wisdom of the past without being bound by it. Each technique, from breath to movement, becomes a tool of empowerment, guiding them toward a life that honors their strength, resilience, and boundless capacity for renewal. Through this process, they emerge not only healed but reborn, embracing the fullness of their experience with grace and clarity.

Chapter 8
Holotropic Breathing

Holotropic breathing stands as one of the most transformative practices within liberation and rebirth therapy, guiding participants to heightened states of awareness and deep personal insight. Developed as a therapeutic practice, holotropic breathing combines controlled breath patterns with evocative music and focused intention to access the subconscious and facilitate profound emotional release. This approach allows participants to bypass the analytical mind, reaching into layers of consciousness typically hidden in everyday awareness. Through this powerful breathing method, participants encounter an immersive journey into the self, where suppressed emotions, forgotten memories, and subconscious insights emerge freely.

In a typical session of holotropic breathing, participants engage in rapid, rhythmic breathing that amplifies oxygen flow, inducing a state of heightened awareness. Unlike traditional breathwork, where breathing is calm and measured, holotropic breathing encourages continuous, active inhales and exhales without pauses. This style of breathing creates an altered state, much like a trance, where the conscious mind releases its usual control and the subconscious rises to the surface. Within this altered state, participants often experience vivid emotions, sensations, and images—fragments of the inner self that have long awaited acknowledgment.

Preparation is key to this practice, as holotropic breathing can bring forth intense experiences. Before beginning, participants are encouraged to set a clear intention, which may focus on releasing a specific emotion, gaining insight into a challenge, or simply opening to whatever the session reveals. This intention serves as a guiding force, anchoring participants through the depths of the experience. Setting this intention requires a degree of openness and trust in the process, an acceptance that whatever arises is part of the healing journey.

The role of music is also central in holotropic breathing sessions. Selected carefully to align with the flow of the breath, music acts as a bridge, evoking emotions and energies that may be inaccessible through breathwork alone. Rhythmic, grounding music often starts the session, supporting the participant's entry into the altered state. As the breathing intensifies, the music shifts to match the heightened emotional and energetic states, often rising to a crescendo, before finally easing into calming, meditative tones that guide participants back to a place of rest. This soundscape mirrors the emotional journey, creating a rhythm that participants can follow as they navigate the layers of their own consciousness.

As the session progresses, participants may experience waves of emotions—grief, joy, anger, or love—that surface without warning. These emotions, unfiltered and raw, are part of the subconscious expression, revealing the body's hidden energetic imprints. In these moments, participants are encouraged to remain present with whatever arises, breathing through the sensations rather than resisting or analyzing them. By staying with the breath, they allow each emotion to crest and fall naturally, moving through the body in a way that feels both liberating and cathartic. This process of breathing through emotions creates a pathway for release, allowing stored energies to be fully expressed and then let go.

Participants also frequently encounter symbolic imagery or memories during holotropic breathing. These may take the form of vivid scenes, archetypal figures, or moments from one's own life, offering insight into aspects of the self that are ready for exploration. Rather than interpreting or analyzing these symbols immediately, participants are guided to experience them fully, absorbing whatever emotional or physical sensations accompany the images. This experience becomes a direct communication with the subconscious, a dialogue where the imagery itself holds the key to understanding and release. Only after the session, through reflection or journaling, does the deeper meaning of these symbols begin to emerge.

Body sensations are another profound aspect of holotropic breathing. The increased oxygen and altered state often produce physical sensations—tingling, warmth, or vibrations—that move through the body. Some participants feel these sensations concentrated in specific areas, such as the heart, hands, or abdomen, signaling where energies are being released. Rather than attempting to control or suppress these sensations, participants are encouraged to lean into them, allowing the body to guide the process. This surrender to the body's impulses is crucial, as it facilitates the movement of blocked energies, creating a sense of release and renewal.

Throughout the process, the support of a trained facilitator is invaluable. Holotropic breathing can evoke powerful emotions and physical responses, and a facilitator provides grounding, guidance, and reassurance. The facilitator's presence ensures a safe environment, where participants feel free to express and explore their inner world fully. Whether through a gentle touch on the shoulder or a calming voice, the facilitator serves as an anchor, a reminder of safety and connection during the most intense moments of the journey.

As the session comes to a close, participants gradually slow their breathing, allowing their consciousness to return to a state of calm. Soft, grounding music eases the transition, creating a safe space for reflection as participants reconnect with the present moment. This transition is gentle and intentional, honoring the depth of the experience and giving the participant time to process any insights or emotions that emerged. A period of silence or quiet contemplation follows, where participants can rest and begin to integrate the experience internally before stepping back into the outside world.

In the realm of holotropic breathing, the breath becomes more than a function of life—it transforms into a tool of liberation, a means of accessing the deepest layers of self and releasing what no longer serves. Each session reveals new dimensions of consciousness, helping participants shed past burdens, embrace healing, and connect with the profound wisdom of their own being. Through holotropic breathing, they enter a state where the mind, body, and spirit converge, opening the door to a powerful and transformative rebirth.

Building upon the foundational techniques of holotropic breathing, this chapter delves deeper into the advanced practices and adaptations that allow participants to tailor the experience to their unique needs and goals. In its essence, holotropic breathing is an intimate journey, where each session offers new layers of insight, release, and transformation. As participants become more familiar with the practice, they are encouraged to explore techniques that enhance their connection to self, deepen emotional release, and adapt holotropic breathing for ongoing personal growth.

Advanced holotropic breathing often involves longer sessions, allowing participants to dive further into the subconscious and access memories or emotions that reside in the deeper layers of the psyche. While a typical session may last an hour, advanced practitioners may extend their breathwork up to two hours, creating an expanded container for inner exploration. This extended time encourages the mind to surrender fully, allowing the participant to bypass the surface-level thoughts and enter a state of profound immersion. In these longer sessions, the body's rhythms become more pronounced, and the breath serves as a continuous thread, guiding the participant deeper into the unfolding experience.

Incorporating personalized intentions into each session becomes even more powerful at this stage. Participants might choose to focus on specific areas of their life where they seek clarity or healing, such as relationships, self-identity, or past traumas. By setting a specific intention, the participant directs their subconscious to bring forth memories, images, or insights related to that theme. The intention acts as a compass, subtly guiding the flow of the experience while allowing the subconscious to reveal information that aligns with the participant's focus. This practice transforms each session into a targeted exploration, amplifying the potential for healing and growth within that area of life.

To further deepen the experience, some practitioners incorporate body mapping into their holotropic breathing practice. Body mapping involves focusing the breath on specific areas within the body that feel tense or energetically charged. As participants breathe into these areas, they may encounter emotions, memories, or sensations tied to those physical regions. This practice helps bring awareness to the mind-body connection, revealing how certain life experiences have influenced specific parts of the body. Through focused breathing, these areas begin to soften, releasing the energy held there and allowing for physical and emotional liberation. Over time, body mapping can uncover hidden layers of trauma or unresolved emotions, which can then be released and integrated.

Visualization is another powerful technique that can be paired with holotropic breathing for a more focused and personalized experience. Participants may visualize their breath as a stream of light, moving through the body and illuminating any areas of tension or darkness. As they breathe, they imagine this light growing brighter, dissolving blockages and bringing clarity to their inner world. Alternatively, some participants envision themselves journeying through symbolic landscapes, such as forests, rivers, or mountains, each representing an aspect of their subconscious. This visualization not only deepens the emotional impact but also allows participants to connect with archetypal symbols, enhancing the sense of meaning and purpose within the experience.

Advanced techniques also include partnered holotropic breathing, a practice where participants engage in breathwork with a trusted partner or facilitator who mirrors their breathing pattern. This mirrored breathing creates an energetic bond, allowing each participant to feel supported and connected throughout the experience. The partner may offer gentle guidance, hold a hand, or simply mirror the rhythm of the breath, providing reassurance and grounding during intense moments. This practice can be especially powerful for those who have difficulty accessing deeper emotional layers on their own, as the presence of a supportive partner creates a safe space for vulnerability and expression.

After an intense holotropic breathing session, integration practices are essential. Participants are encouraged to spend time in quiet reflection, allowing the insights and emotions from the session to settle within the conscious mind. Journaling serves as a powerful integration tool, where participants can capture the themes, symbols, and revelations that surfaced. Writing about the experience brings clarity to the subconscious messages, helping to translate abstract emotions and symbols into concrete insights that can guide one's life. This written reflection also provides a record of the participant's journey, allowing them to revisit their experiences over time and observe their personal growth.

In addition to journaling, creative expression can play an important role in the integration process. Participants may feel inspired to draw, paint, or even create music based on the imagery or emotions that emerged during the session. This creative process allows the subconscious to express itself freely, beyond the limitations of language, helping to release any remaining energies and bring a sense of completion to the session. Through art, participants often find new layers of meaning and insight that further enrich their understanding of the experience.

Grounding practices are equally essential, especially after deep sessions that involve intense emotional release. Walking in nature, focusing on the sensation of the earth beneath one's feet, or engaging in gentle stretching can help the body recalibrate and return to a state of balance. Grounding reconnects participants with the present moment, allowing them to carry the lessons from their holotropic experience into their everyday lives. As they return to their daily routines, grounding practices provide a sense of stability, reinforcing that they are fully rooted in their body, safe, and ready to integrate their new insights.

For those who wish to continue with holotropic breathing as a regular practice, developing a personal ritual or routine can deepen the experience over time. This might include preparing the space with intentional objects such as candles, crystals, or symbols that hold meaning, signaling to the subconscious that it is time for introspection and release. As holotropic breathing becomes a consistent practice, participants may notice an increased sensitivity to their inner world, finding that their awareness of self deepens both within and beyond the session.

Ultimately, advanced holotropic breathing is a journey into the innermost realms of the psyche, offering the potential for healing, insight, and transformation. By cultivating trust in the breath, participants unlock a powerful tool that guides them through the complexities of their own consciousness, revealing the wisdom and strength that reside within. With each session, they draw closer to the essence of self, transcending old limitations and experiencing the profound rebirth that awaits within the expansive depths of the soul. Through this journey, they find a renewed sense of wholeness, empowered by the knowledge that the path to liberation lies within each breath.

Chapter 9
Overcoming Limiting Mental Patterns

Limiting mental patterns are unseen forces that shape how one perceives, interacts with, and experiences the world. These patterns, formed through past experiences, beliefs, and social conditioning, often operate below conscious awareness, subtly influencing decisions, behaviors, and self-perception. In the journey of liberation and rebirth, identifying and overcoming these patterns is crucial, as they are often the mental barriers that keep one from accessing inner freedom and true self-expression. Recognizing these limitations is the first step in breaking free from their hold and realigning the mind with a more empowering, liberated state.

One of the fundamental concepts in this work is understanding how limiting beliefs form. Often rooted in early life experiences, these beliefs arise as coping mechanisms or interpretations of significant events. For example, repeated experiences of rejection can lead to a belief that one is unworthy of love, or challenging circumstances may create a fear-based mindset that constantly anticipates failure. These beliefs take on a life of their own, shaping how one interacts with others and sees themselves. By bringing these beliefs to light, participants begin to see that these patterns, once protective or comforting, no longer serve them on the path to growth and rebirth.

The process of identifying these mental patterns requires a heightened sense of self-awareness. Participants are encouraged to pay attention to recurring thoughts, self-talk, and reactions to specific triggers. Negative self-talk—such as thoughts of inadequacy or failure—is often a signpost pointing to a deeper limiting belief. For instance, the thought "I can't do this" might reveal an underlying belief of incompetence or unworthiness. Through this reflective practice, participants start to map out their mental landscape, recognizing areas where these patterns hold sway and limit their potential.

Journaling is a powerful tool in this phase, as it allows participants to capture and analyze their internal dialogue. By writing down recurring thoughts and exploring their origins, participants create a map of their mental patterns, identifying the beliefs that have shaped their worldview. This written record reveals patterns that may have gone unnoticed, allowing participants to trace each belief back to its roots. Often, the simple act of writing these thoughts brings a new level of clarity, enabling participants to see these patterns not as truths, but as constructs of the mind that can be reshaped and released.

Visualization offers another technique for identifying and challenging limiting beliefs. Participants are invited to close their eyes and visualize a moment when they felt held back by a particular belief, such as a fear of failure or rejection. They are encouraged to observe the emotions, physical sensations, and thoughts that arise in this memory, without judgment. By revisiting these moments in a controlled, intentional way, participants can observe how these beliefs have influenced their behavior and choices. This exercise creates a space for reflection, where participants see the belief for what it is—a thought pattern that can be challenged and changed.

Once limiting patterns are identified, participants begin the work of releasing and replacing them with more empowering beliefs. Affirmations serve as a bridge between old beliefs and new, more constructive patterns. For example, a participant who struggles with self-doubt might adopt an affirmation like "I am capable and worthy of success." Through daily repetition, these affirmations begin to rewrite the subconscious mind, creating a new internal narrative that reinforces confidence and resilience. This practice is not a quick fix but a gradual process, as the mind slowly replaces old, restrictive beliefs with thoughts that align with one's potential and inner strength.

Another powerful method in overcoming limiting beliefs is cognitive restructuring, a process where participants actively challenge and reframe their thoughts. This technique encourages individuals to question the validity of their beliefs by asking, "Is this belief absolutely true?" or "What evidence do I have to support or refute this belief?" By engaging in this inquiry, participants begin to see that many of their beliefs are based on assumptions or past experiences that no longer apply. This questioning opens the mind to alternative perspectives, helping participants adopt a more balanced and constructive outlook on themselves and their potential.

Mindfulness meditation also plays a role in breaking free from limiting patterns, as it helps participants observe their thoughts without attachment or judgment. In meditation, participants are guided to focus on the present moment, watching their thoughts as they arise and pass. This practice creates distance between the self and the thoughts, allowing participants to see that they are not defined by their mental patterns. With time, mindfulness reduces the power of limiting beliefs by weakening their emotional hold, enabling participants to approach life with greater openness and curiosity.

In addition to these practices, grounding techniques such as body awareness exercises bring participants back to the present moment, reinforcing that they are safe and capable in the here and now. Body awareness helps counteract the negative energy that often accompanies limiting beliefs, providing an immediate sense of calm and clarity. Through grounding, participants regain control over their mental state, reminding themselves that they can choose how to respond to their thoughts, rather than letting old patterns dictate their responses.

As participants continue this process, they come to understand that limiting beliefs are not permanent fixtures but fluid constructs shaped by experiences and interpretations. Through self-awareness, mindfulness, and cognitive restructuring, they begin to break down these mental barriers, revealing a mindset that is expansive, open, and aligned with their true self. By overcoming limiting patterns, participants create the mental foundation necessary for a liberated and empowered life, stepping into a version of themselves that is ready to embrace growth, connection, and inner freedom. In this shift, they unlock a profound sense of potential, moving forward with a mind no longer confined by the past, but fully present and attuned to the possibilities that lie ahead.

Having recognized and begun to dismantle limiting mental patterns, participants now deepen their practice by replacing these old beliefs with empowering thoughts and behaviors that align with their true potential. This stage is a conscious reconstruction, where each thought, habit, and belief is chosen with awareness and intention. The process transforms the mind from a reactive space into a creative one, enabling participants to cultivate mental resilience, confidence, and self-compassion.

One foundational technique in this phase is the development of counter-beliefs—new, empowering beliefs that directly challenge and replace limiting patterns. For each limiting belief identified, participants are encouraged to create a counter-belief that affirms their strengths and potential. For example, if a participant has the limiting belief, "I'm not good enough," they may replace it with the counter-belief, "I have unique strengths and am worthy of success." By consciously choosing beliefs that reflect their aspirations and values, participants begin to reframe their inner dialogue, creating a foundation of self-worth and possibility.

Daily affirmations reinforce these new beliefs, helping them take root in the subconscious mind. To deepen the impact, participants can pair affirmations with visualization, imagining themselves embodying these empowering beliefs. For instance, while repeating "I am resilient and capable," a participant might visualize themselves confidently handling a challenging situation, feeling the sense of strength and composure that this belief brings. Visualization brings these affirmations to life, transforming abstract concepts into lived experiences that resonate within the mind and body. Through repetition, these mental exercises shift the subconscious, embedding the new beliefs as the foundation for thought and action.

Journaling continues to serve as a powerful tool for solidifying these shifts. Participants are encouraged to record moments when they actively counter limiting beliefs, noting the impact of these new perspectives on their experiences and emotions. By reflecting on these moments, they begin to see tangible evidence of their transformation, witnessing how shifting their beliefs affects their behavior and interactions. This practice of reflection reinforces the reality of their growth, creating a written narrative of change that provides encouragement and clarity as they progress.

In addition to affirmations and journaling, embodiment practices play a vital role in reinforcing empowering mental patterns. Participants are guided to align their posture, movement, and breathing with their new beliefs. For example, if one is working to cultivate confidence, they might stand tall, with shoulders back and head held high, adopting the physical expression of confidence. Similarly, breathing deeply and steadily can evoke feelings of calm and control, even in challenging situations. These embodiment practices create a physiological connection to the mental shifts, making the new beliefs not only intellectual but also experiential, rooted in the body as well as the mind.

To further deepen these empowering beliefs, participants engage in self-compassion exercises. This practice involves treating oneself with kindness, understanding, and patience, especially when faced with setbacks or doubts. Self-compassion practices include gently acknowledging and reframing critical self-talk, offering oneself words of encouragement, and embracing imperfections as part of the growth process. By cultivating self-compassion, participants replace self-criticism with self-acceptance, creating an internal environment that nurtures resilience and fosters a healthy mindset.

Mindfulness meditation continues to be a cornerstone of this process, as it helps participants observe and gently release any lingering attachments to old patterns. Through regular meditation, they become adept at recognizing thoughts as they arise, without judgment or attachment. By observing these thoughts without reaction, participants learn to distinguish between the true self and transient mental patterns, reinforcing the understanding that limiting beliefs are constructs that no longer hold power. In this way, mindfulness meditation helps integrate new mental patterns, fostering a mindset that is grounded in present-moment awareness and free from the influence of past conditioning.

To ensure lasting change, participants also learn to incorporate empowering beliefs into their daily lives through intentional actions. This practice involves identifying situations where limiting patterns might previously have surfaced and consciously choosing actions that reflect the new beliefs. For example, if a participant's new belief is "I am worthy of love and respect," they may begin setting healthy boundaries or expressing their needs in relationships. Each intentional action reinforces the new belief, transforming it from an internal mantra into a lived reality. Over time, these actions accumulate, creating a life that reflects the mental patterns aligned with the participant's true self.

Supportive community interactions, such as sharing insights with trusted peers or mentors, can further strengthen these mental shifts. By discussing their experiences and challenges in a safe space, participants receive validation and encouragement, reinforcing their belief in their own progress. This exchange fosters accountability and mutual support, creating an environment where each participant's growth is seen and celebrated. As they witness others also overcoming limiting beliefs, participants gain confidence in their own transformation, seeing that change is not only possible but already unfolding.

Finally, creating a personal ritual to close each day serves as a reminder of the progress made. This ritual might include reflecting on one empowering action taken, expressing gratitude for one's resilience, or visualizing the day ahead with confidence and positivity. This daily ritual becomes a grounding practice that marks each day as a step toward the liberated self, providing a gentle yet consistent reminder of the journey's purpose and direction.

Through these practices, participants transcend the mental patterns that once confined them, embracing beliefs that support their growth and self-expression. With each new thought, affirmation, and action, they shape a reality that aligns with their potential, empowered to move through life with resilience and authenticity. The mind, once a space filled with doubt and limitation, becomes a canvas upon which they paint their own vision, creating a life rooted in liberation, strength, and inner peace. In this renewed mental landscape, they step forward not only transformed but fully empowered, free to embrace the journey ahead.

Chapter 10
Somatic Integration in Rituals

In the journey of liberation and rebirth, the body is not only a vessel for experience but a vital participant in the process of transformation. Somatic integration emphasizes the role of the body as an anchor for emotional, mental, and spiritual growth, recognizing that the mind and body work together to process, release, and embody change. Through somatic practices, participants establish a connection between their physical sensations and inner experiences, allowing them to deepen their awareness, release stored tension, and fully integrate the healing process.

The concept of somatic integration is rooted in the belief that the body holds memories and emotions that influence our responses and behaviors. These stored energies, often unconscious, manifest as physical tension, postures, or even chronic discomfort. In somatic integration, participants learn to tune into these sensations, observing them as expressions of the subconscious. This mindful attention helps bring awareness to areas of the body that may feel heavy, tense, or numb, as these often correspond to emotional blockages or unresolved experiences.

One foundational practice in somatic integration is body scanning, a technique where participants bring focused awareness to each part of their body, from the toes to the top of the head. This scanning process allows them to identify areas of tightness, warmth, tingling, or any sensation that stands out. By acknowledging and breathing into these sensations, participants begin to unlock emotions held within the body. For instance, a tightness in the chest might reveal feelings of grief, while tension in the jaw may connect to unexpressed anger or frustration. Body scanning thus serves as a gateway, connecting physical sensations with deeper emotional layers.

Another essential technique is grounding, which involves connecting the body to the earth to create a sense of stability and safety. Grounding practices, such as standing barefoot on the earth or visualizing roots extending from the feet deep into the ground, help participants feel anchored and present. This grounded state is essential for somatic work, as it allows participants to explore intense emotions without feeling overwhelmed or disconnected. As they feel rooted and supported by the earth, they find the courage to explore and release sensations and emotions within the body, confident in their ability to remain steady through the process.

Breathwork, a vital component of somatic integration, acts as a bridge between the body and mind. Different breath patterns can evoke various emotional responses, allowing participants to access memories and sensations stored in the body. Deep, rhythmic breathing can help release tension and encourage relaxation, while more intense breathing patterns can bring to the surface emotions or memories buried within. As participants breathe deeply into areas of tension, they may feel energy shift, releasing emotional blockages and creating a sense of openness and ease. This practice strengthens the mind-body connection, enabling the breath to serve as a guide through the somatic landscape of the self.

Movement, too, becomes a powerful tool for somatic integration. Participants are encouraged to engage in gentle, intuitive movement, allowing the body to stretch, sway, or flow in response to inner sensations. This movement may be as simple as swaying side to side or as dynamic as dancing. By letting the body move naturally, participants begin to release the tension held in muscles and tissues, often experiencing a sense of liberation. Movement in somatic integration is not about structure or form; it is about giving the body permission to express itself, to follow the impulses that arise naturally as energies shift and release.

Touch is another profound element in somatic practices. Whether placing a hand over the heart, gently massaging tense areas, or simply holding one's own hands, touch acts as a nurturing gesture that communicates care and safety to the body. Participants may place their hands on areas of discomfort or tension, sending warmth and compassion to these places. This act of self-touch creates a feeling of reassurance, calming the nervous system and facilitating emotional release. Through touch, participants reconnect with their own physical presence, cultivating a sense of self-compassion and acceptance.

Journaling after each somatic session provides an avenue to reflect on and integrate the experience. Participants are encouraged to document the sensations, emotions, and insights that arose during the practice, noting any connections between body sensations and emotional memories. This reflective process allows participants to make sense of their experiences, observing patterns over time and gaining insight into the ways their body communicates its needs. These journal entries become a record of growth, helping participants see how somatic practices reveal and transform parts of the self that were previously hidden.

In addition, visualization techniques complement somatic integration, as participants are guided to imagine their body filled with a healing light or flowing energy. They may visualize this light moving through tense areas, gradually dissolving blockages or soothing discomfort. Visualization enhances the physical sensations experienced during somatic practices, adding a layer of mental focus that deepens the release process. This imagery reinforces the participant's sense of connection to their body, creating a unified experience of mind, body, and spirit working together toward healing.

Somatic integration is a journey of reclaiming the body's wisdom, teaching participants to listen and respond to its subtle messages. Through these practices, they begin to see the body as a guide, an ally that holds valuable insights into their emotions, memories, and patterns. Each sensation, each breath, and each movement becomes a step closer to wholeness, where the mind and body are no longer separate but harmoniously connected.

In this harmonious state, participants experience the body not as a passive vessel but as a dynamic, responsive partner in the journey of liberation and rebirth. Somatic integration allows them to inhabit their bodies with presence and compassion, embracing every sensation as part of their unfolding story. Through this connection, they anchor themselves in the present, prepared to continue the path toward deeper self-awareness and transformation.

As the practice of somatic integration deepens, participants explore techniques that amplify their connection to the body's wisdom, helping them achieve a more profound and complete rebirth experience. This stage of integration builds on foundational practices by inviting participants to engage in advanced techniques that foster an even richer dialogue between mind and body, unveiling layers of insight and release that extend beyond conscious awareness. Through these methods, participants learn to navigate the complexities of their physical and emotional landscapes, embracing the body as an active partner in transformation.

One advanced approach in somatic integration is focused energy flow, where participants direct their attention to specific areas of the body to release deeply embedded emotions or tensions. This practice begins with a mindful scan of the body, noting areas that feel tense, numb, or overly energized. Participants then concentrate their breath, awareness, and even gentle touch on these areas, inviting the energy to soften and shift. For instance, if a participant identifies a sense of heaviness in the chest, they might envision each inhale filling this area with light, warmth, or a sense of release, and each exhale carrying away any heaviness. This targeted focus fosters a powerful release of long-held energy, creating space for new emotional clarity and physical ease.

Sound vibration is another technique that enhances the somatic process by introducing resonance within the body. Through humming, chanting, or toning specific sounds, participants experience how vibration moves through the body, often reaching areas where words and conscious thought cannot. The low hum of "OM" or the gentle tone of "AH" resonates through different body parts, breaking up energetic blocks and fostering a sense of harmony within. These sounds align with specific energy centers, creating subtle vibrations that facilitate emotional and physical release. The sound acts as a bridge, connecting mind and body in a profound dialogue that transcends language, bringing about healing through resonance.

Sensory grounding adds another layer to somatic integration, using physical objects to root participants firmly in the present moment. Holding stones, placing one's hands on cool earth, or feeling the texture of fabric against the skin are simple yet powerful practices that bring awareness back to the senses. This practice is particularly effective during intense emotional releases, offering a steady, grounding presence that reminds participants of their connection to the physical world. As they focus on these sensory experiences, participants find a balance between the intensity of inner exploration and the comfort of the tangible, reinforcing their ability to navigate difficult emotions with presence and stability.

Partnered bodywork, when done with a trusted partner or facilitator, is another advanced technique that can deepen somatic integration. In this practice, the participant and partner work together through gentle touch, pressure, or guided movement. This approach invites a supportive presence into the process, helping the participant feel safe and held as they explore physical and emotional tensions. For example, the partner might place their hands on the participant's shoulders, applying gentle pressure that encourages the release of tension stored there. This supportive touch not only fosters trust but also allows participants to experience the healing power of connection, as the presence of another helps amplify their own awareness and release.

Guided movement meditation, often using slow, intuitive movements, enhances body-mind awareness by allowing participants to express emotions physically. In this practice, participants are invited to explore any movements that feel natural or necessary in response to inner sensations, without concern for structure or technique. Movement becomes a language, a way for the body to express what words cannot convey. Some may find themselves stretching, twisting, or even gently rocking, each movement helping to release stored energies or feelings that have no verbal expression. This unstructured movement not only frees the body but also encourages participants to trust their body's intuitive impulses, strengthening the bond between mind and body.

Somatic journaling serves as a reflective tool for integrating these advanced somatic practices, allowing participants to capture the physical sensations and emotions they experienced in a session. This form of journaling focuses on bodily sensations—describing textures, temperatures, or tensions felt in different areas. For example, a participant may write about "a tightness in the throat that softened with each breath" or "a warmth that spread through the chest." This detailed record helps them understand the messages their body communicates, uncovering patterns over time that reveal deeper aspects of their healing journey.

Visualization techniques that align with energy centers, or chakras, add depth to somatic work. Participants may visualize each chakra as a glowing sphere of light, moving their focus from the base of the spine up to the crown of the head, pausing at each center to observe sensations, colors, or emotions that arise. This visualization allows participants to detect blockages or imbalances, guiding them to areas that may need further attention or release. As they visualize these centers, participants often experience a balancing effect, harmonizing mind, body, and spirit and creating a clear flow of energy that supports the rebirth process.

Finally, ritual closure is essential in advanced somatic integration, as it provides participants with a sense of completion and grounding. This closure can include a series of intentional breaths, a brief gratitude practice, or a simple gesture such as placing a hand over the heart to acknowledge the body's role in the journey. This act honors the process, allowing the participant to recognize their growth and transformation, marking the moment as sacred. Ritual closure reinforces the participant's connection to their body and the progress they have made, grounding the insights gained so they carry forward into daily life.

Through these advanced techniques, participants learn to fully inhabit their bodies, integrating every part of themselves into the journey of liberation and rebirth. The body, once seen as a mere vessel, becomes a guide and a partner, revealing wisdom, resilience, and strength that enhance the transformative process. Somatic integration offers participants the chance to move beyond intellectual understanding, connecting them to the core of their own being. Through each breath, movement, and sensation, they embrace the path to wholeness, experiencing rebirth not only as a concept but as a lived reality within every fiber of their being.

Chapter 11
Stages of Emotional Healing

Emotional healing unfolds in stages, each phase revealing a unique layer of self-awareness and liberation. This journey through the stages of healing is a deeply personal one, where participants encounter and work through their emotional landscape. In liberation and rebirth therapy, understanding these stages offers clarity and assurance, illuminating a path that may otherwise feel challenging and unfamiliar. As participants move through these stages, they gradually reconnect with their essence, shedding past burdens and aligning with a truer, lighter self.

The first stage of emotional healing is acknowledgment. In this phase, participants recognize the emotions that have been buried or ignored. Often, these emotions manifest as recurring thoughts, unexplained moods, or physical discomfort. By becoming aware of these signals, participants bring unconscious feelings into conscious awareness, acknowledging their presence without judgment. Acknowledgment is a courageous step, as it requires participants to confront aspects of their emotional lives that may be uncomfortable. However, this stage is foundational, as it initiates the process of healing, allowing emotions to move from repression into conscious awareness.

The next stage is acceptance, where participants allow themselves to fully feel and accept their emotions, rather than resisting or suppressing them. Acceptance involves a deep sense of self-compassion, creating a safe internal space for all emotions, including those that may feel unpleasant or difficult. In this stage, participants may confront emotions such as anger, sadness, or fear, approaching them not as problems to be solved but as natural aspects of the human experience. By cultivating this acceptance, participants dissolve the barriers that keep these emotions locked within, allowing them to flow freely without being judged or resisted.

Following acceptance comes the stage of exploration, where participants delve deeper into the origins and nature of their emotions. Through self-reflection, journaling, and guided introspection, they explore the roots of their feelings, seeking to understand the experiences, memories, or beliefs that have contributed to their emotional patterns. In this phase, participants may revisit past events or relationships that hold emotional significance, allowing them to trace their current feelings back to their source. This exploration offers valuable insight, revealing the connections between past experiences and present emotions, helping participants see how certain patterns have shaped their lives.

The fourth stage, release, is an active process of letting go. Once participants have acknowledged, accepted, and explored their emotions, they are ready to release the energy held within them. This release can take many forms—breathwork, movement, sound, or even creative expression—each allowing emotions to leave the body and mind. In this stage, participants may experience a physical sensation of relief or lightness, as though a weight has been lifted. Release is a powerful phase, where the emotional energies that once felt heavy or restrictive dissolve, making space for new, lighter energies to flow.

After releasing comes the stage of integration, where participants consolidate the insights gained from the previous stages, creating a harmonious inner landscape. Integration involves reflecting on the journey through acknowledgment, acceptance, exploration, and release, observing how each stage has contributed to a greater understanding of self. Participants may use journaling, meditation, or visualization to reflect on these shifts, grounding the experience within their daily lives. This stage of integration reinforces the healing process, allowing participants to embody the growth and freedom they have achieved.

Finally, the journey reaches the stage of renewal, where participants emerge from the healing process with a fresh perspective. Renewal is the embodiment of emotional liberation, a sense of clarity and openness that comes from having shed the emotional weights of the past. In this stage, participants feel an expanded sense of self, aligned with their essence and ready to move forward unburdened. Renewal is not only a moment of emotional relief but a rebirth—a chance to experience life from a place of freedom, authenticity, and inner peace.

Each of these stages requires patience and self-compassion, as emotional healing is rarely a linear journey. Participants may revisit certain stages multiple times, encountering layers of emotions they were not initially aware of. By understanding these stages, they approach the process with greater clarity, trusting that each phase serves a purpose in the broader journey of healing and transformation.

Through this journey, participants experience emotional healing not as an abstract concept but as a lived transformation that brings them closer to their essence. With each stage, they release the past and embrace the present, forging a path that leads not only to healing but to a profound rebirth of the self.

As participants deepen their experience in the stages of emotional healing, they encounter advanced techniques that allow them to access and work through deeper layers of emotional experience. Each stage offers an opportunity not only for awareness and release but also for profound transformation and integration. Moving beyond initial acknowledgment and acceptance, these advanced practices serve as tools to help participants explore, release, and renew with a depth that resonates within every aspect of their lives.

In the acknowledgment stage, advanced techniques such as emotional tracking allow participants to identify and understand their emotions with precision. Emotional tracking involves actively observing the emotions that arise throughout the day, especially in response to specific situations or interactions. By noting when and where certain feelings appear, participants become attuned to their emotional landscape, noticing patterns and triggers that may previously have gone unnoticed. This practice allows them to approach their emotions with curiosity, recognizing each feeling as an invitation to greater self-understanding.

During the acceptance stage, participants are encouraged to practice radical self-compassion. This approach goes beyond basic self-acceptance, inviting participants to embrace every emotion as part of their humanity, without conditions or restrictions. Radical self-compassion means offering oneself unconditional kindness, even when faced with emotions that feel overwhelming. Participants may place a hand over their heart, repeat affirming phrases, or simply breathe deeply as they hold space for their emotions. Through this practice, they foster a compassionate inner dialogue, releasing the need to judge or alter their feelings and instead embracing them fully, allowing acceptance to flow without resistance.

In the exploration stage, techniques such as guided emotional inquiry bring greater depth to self-reflection. In this practice, participants ask targeted questions about their emotions to uncover underlying beliefs, memories, or influences. Questions like "What does this emotion want me to know?" or "Where does this feeling come from?" open a doorway to understanding the roots of each emotion. This inquiry often brings forth memories or insights that reveal the origins of recurring patterns, helping participants connect the dots between past experiences and present feelings. Guided inquiry encourages participants to see their emotions not as isolated reactions but as part of a larger, interconnected narrative.

The release stage becomes a powerful point of transformation with practices like cathartic movement and expressive sound. Cathartic movement encourages participants to move their body freely, using dance, shaking, or stretching to release pent-up emotions. This movement is unstructured, allowing participants to follow the body's impulses as it expresses and releases. Expressive sound—whether through chanting, toning, or simply vocalizing—allows emotions to be released audibly, bypassing mental resistance. These practices transform release into a physical and vocal experience, offering participants a profound sense of liberation as they let go of emotional energies held within the body.

To deepen the integration stage, participants engage in practices such as visualization and embodiment. Through visualization, they imagine themselves embodying the new insights and emotional freedom they have gained. For example, a participant might envision a warm light filling their chest, symbolizing the release of sadness, or imagine themselves walking with confidence, free from past burdens. Embodiment involves bringing this visualization into daily actions—practicing speaking, moving, or even breathing as if the insights gained during healing are already part of who they are. These practices bridge the inner experience with the external world, reinforcing the transformation as participants carry their growth into everyday life.

The stage of renewal is enriched by rituals that celebrate and affirm the rebirth participants experience. This stage can include creating a personal ritual—lighting a candle, meditating on their journey, or writing a letter to their past self—that honors the healing process and marks a new beginning. Renewal rituals symbolize the conclusion of one phase and the start of another, helping participants feel the magnitude of their transformation. As they consciously celebrate the journey they've undertaken, they step fully into their new sense of self, with a mind, heart, and spirit aligned with peace and freedom.

Advanced emotional healing is a continuous unfolding, revealing layers of growth and transformation as participants revisit these stages. With each round of acknowledgment, acceptance, exploration, release, integration, and renewal, they move closer to a state of wholeness. In this profound journey, they find not only healing but also a sense of empowerment, clarity, and inner peace that enables them to live with authenticity and openness. This journey through the stages of emotional healing becomes the foundation for true rebirth, as participants emerge transformed and ready to embrace life with a renewed spirit and unwavering resilience.

Chapter 12
Therapeutic Guidance

Guiding others through liberation and rebirth is a sacred role, one that calls for deep empathy, patience, and an understanding of the healing process. As a therapeutic guide, one serves as a steady presence, helping individuals navigate the complexities of emotional release, self-discovery, and transformation. The role is not about directing or influencing the participant's path but about creating a safe and compassionate space that allows each individual to explore their journey at their own pace. In this chapter, we delve into the foundational principles of therapeutic guidance, emphasizing presence, active listening, and creating an environment where participants feel seen, heard, and supported.

At the core of therapeutic guidance lies the concept of holding space, an act of being fully present with another's experiences without judgment or interruption. Holding space means providing a calm and receptive environment where participants feel free to express their emotions, no matter how intense or vulnerable. The guide remains centered, attentive, and open, allowing the participant's process to unfold naturally. This presence creates a sense of safety, encouraging participants to delve into emotions or memories they may have previously resisted. The guide's role is to witness, honor, and support, creating an atmosphere of acceptance that fosters trust and healing.

Active listening is equally crucial in therapeutic guidance. This is a practice of listening deeply—not only to words but to tone, emotion, and body language. When participants share their experiences, the guide listens without formulating responses or solutions. Instead, they mirror the participant's emotions, perhaps by summarizing what they've heard, acknowledging the feelings expressed, or simply maintaining eye contact and an empathetic posture. This form of listening allows the participant to feel genuinely heard, validating their experiences and affirming their emotions. Active listening helps the guide understand not only the participant's words but also the underlying layers of their experience, providing a foundation for compassionate support.

Creating a sacred space is another essential component of therapeutic guidance. A sacred space is a physical and energetic environment where participants feel comfortable and secure. This might involve arranging a private, calm setting with soft lighting, soothing sounds, or objects like candles, cushions, or crystals that evoke a sense of peace. By intentionally preparing the space, the guide helps set the tone for introspection, signaling that this is a dedicated time and place for healing. The sacredness of the space reminds participants that their journey is meaningful, encouraging them to explore their inner world with a sense of respect and reverence.

The guide's energy and demeanor play a vital role in therapeutic guidance. Remaining grounded and calm, the guide serves as an anchor during moments of intense emotion or release. Techniques such as mindful breathing, maintaining a gentle voice, and projecting warmth help the guide maintain a steady presence. By embodying calmness and empathy, the guide subtly encourages participants to feel comfortable with their own emotions, no matter how vulnerable or powerful. This steady energy acts as a stabilizing force, helping participants feel safe as they navigate their emotions and experiences.

Another critical aspect of therapeutic guidance is non-judgmental support. The guide approaches each session without preconceived notions or expectations, allowing the participant's journey to unfold authentically. Non-judgmental support means accepting all emotions, reactions, and experiences without labeling them as "good" or "bad." Whether the participant expresses anger, sorrow, confusion, or joy, the guide remains open, supporting them without attempting to redirect or change their process. This acceptance empowers participants to explore their full range of emotions, knowing they are free to express themselves without fear of judgment.

Guides also learn to work with silence as a therapeutic tool. Silence provides a space for participants to process their thoughts, allowing emotions and insights to emerge without interruption. Rather than rushing to fill quiet moments, the guide embraces these pauses, understanding that silence often invites deeper reflection. In moments of silence, participants may feel encouraged to explore thoughts or feelings that are just beginning to surface, giving them the time and space they need to connect with their inner self. Through this approach, silence becomes an ally in the healing process, creating room for the participant's own insights to unfold.

Boundaries are equally essential in therapeutic guidance, ensuring a respectful and balanced relationship. Setting clear boundaries helps both guide and participant understand their roles and responsibilities, creating a professional and respectful dynamic. Boundaries might include clear guidelines about session duration, confidentiality, and respectful communication. By establishing these boundaries, the guide models self-respect and reinforces the participant's sense of safety within the therapeutic relationship. Boundaries also help the guide maintain their own energy and well-being, allowing them to remain present and effective in their role.

In therapeutic guidance, the guide must also cultivate self-awareness, constantly reflecting on their own emotions, biases, and reactions. Self-awareness allows the guide to recognize when personal experiences or assumptions might influence their role, enabling them to stay fully present and unbiased. Practices such as mindfulness, journaling, and peer support help guides maintain their own clarity, ensuring that their presence remains grounded and open. This self-reflection enables the guide to serve authentically, as they continue to grow alongside the participants they support.

Therapeutic guidance is an art, a compassionate practice that nurtures growth and healing through presence, respect, and unconditional support. By mastering the principles of holding space, active listening, and non-judgmental support, guides become conduits of healing, creating environments where participants feel safe to explore, express, and transform. The guide's presence becomes a reminder that, in this journey of liberation and rebirth, each participant is supported, honored, and deeply valued. Through this sacred role, therapeutic guidance serves as a pathway to profound self-discovery, helping individuals move closer to their own wholeness, free to explore the depths of their inner world with courage and trust.

As the role of therapeutic guidance deepens, advanced techniques and practices become essential in helping participants navigate the more profound layers of liberation and rebirth. Beyond offering a steady presence, the guide learns to respond to each individual's unique needs, adapting their approach to facilitate emotional release, insight, and integration. These advanced techniques focus on fostering a safe, empowering environment where participants can journey through complex emotions and challenging memories, with the guide as both witness and support.

One of the key advanced skills in therapeutic guidance is mirroring. Mirroring involves reflecting the participant's words, emotions, and body language back to them, providing an opportunity for self-recognition. By gently mirroring a participant's posture, tone, or expressions, the guide creates a subtle resonance that helps the participant feel seen and understood. This reflective approach can also help participants become more aware of their own emotions and behaviors, offering insights they may not have noticed on their own. Mirroring is delicate work; it requires sensitivity and attunement, as the guide must balance reflection with respect for the participant's boundaries and comfort.

Guided imagery serves as another powerful tool for advanced therapeutic guidance. This technique involves helping participants visualize settings, objects, or symbols that evoke specific emotions or memories. For example, if a participant is working through feelings of grief, the guide might lead them in visualizing a safe, comforting space where they can connect with and release those emotions. Through guided imagery, participants access parts of their subconscious in a non-threatening way, allowing memories and emotions to surface naturally. This practice helps bridge the conscious and subconscious mind, facilitating a deeper exploration of self that often leads to profound healing.

In moments of intense emotional release, the guide's role expands to include emotional anchoring. Anchoring involves grounding participants during challenging moments, helping them stay connected to the present as they process difficult emotions. Techniques such as encouraging steady, rhythmic breathing, guiding participants to focus on their physical surroundings, or gently reminding them of their strength and resilience all serve to anchor them through the process. By anchoring participants in the present, the guide helps them feel safe and stable, preventing emotional overwhelm and encouraging a balanced release.

As participants confront memories or emotions that may feel overwhelming, the practice of containment becomes essential. Containment provides participants with a way to hold and process intense emotions without becoming flooded by them. The guide may teach participants visualization techniques to "contain" their emotions in an imagined vessel, such as a box or container, which they can revisit in future sessions. This visualization helps participants manage strong feelings without suppressing them, offering a sense of control as they work through complex emotions. Containment becomes a valuable tool, allowing participants to feel empowered even when facing difficult memories or sensations.

Empathic validation is another advanced practice, where the guide actively acknowledges and affirms the participant's experiences and feelings. In validation, the guide may use phrases such as, "It's completely understandable that you feel this way," or "Your feelings are valid." This approach reassures participants that their emotions are real, understandable, and acceptable, helping to dismantle any internalized shame or self-judgment. By receiving validation, participants are encouraged to feel their emotions without resistance, understanding that their experiences are legitimate and that they are not alone in their journey.

In advanced therapeutic guidance, the concept of boundary setting takes on a new depth. Participants working through intense emotions may unconsciously seek more closeness or reassurance from the guide, sometimes blurring the professional boundaries that maintain a therapeutic space. The guide learns to gently reinforce these boundaries, reminding participants of the structure and roles within the session. This boundary-setting is an act of care, helping participants develop emotional resilience and self-sufficiency. By modeling healthy boundaries, the guide supports participants in cultivating self-trust and independence, empowering them to carry their healing into their lives beyond the therapeutic space.

The practice of reflective questioning allows the guide to invite participants into deeper self-inquiry without imposing interpretations or conclusions. Reflective questions are open-ended, designed to help participants explore their emotions, thoughts, and beliefs further. For example, questions like "What does this feeling tell you about yourself?" or "How do you feel this experience has shaped you?" open up space for self-reflection and insight. Reflective questioning honors the participant's autonomy, encouraging them to find their own meanings and insights as they journey inward. This technique fosters an environment where participants can engage in active self-discovery, guided by their own intuition and understanding.

Closing rituals become vital at the end of each session, helping participants transition from the therapeutic space back into daily life. A closing ritual might include a few moments of silent reflection, a grounding breath exercise, or a brief gratitude practice. This ritual honors the participant's courage and journey, marking the session's conclusion in a way that feels complete. Closing rituals provide a sense of closure, allowing participants to carry their insights forward while feeling grounded and supported.

Guides must also practice self-care and reflection as an integral part of their role. The depth of emotional work involved in therapeutic guidance requires the guide to maintain their own well-being to support participants effectively. Self-care practices such as meditation, journaling, or peer supervision sessions allow guides to process their experiences, maintaining emotional clarity and resilience. Through this self-care, the guide remains balanced and fully present, embodying the strength and empathy needed to support participants on their path of healing.

Advanced therapeutic guidance is an art of balancing presence with technique, intuition with skill. By refining these practices, guides cultivate an environment where participants feel empowered to explore their inner world, navigate emotional landscapes, and discover the resilience that lies within. Through empathy, respect, and skilled support, therapeutic guides become catalysts for transformation, helping individuals find healing and rebirth within themselves. This journey of guidance is one of mutual growth, where the guide and participant alike are touched by the profound power of liberation and self-discovery.

Chapter 13
Higher Self and Inner Wisdom

Connection with the Higher Self is one of the most transformative aspects of liberation and rebirth therapy. This inner guide embodies our purest essence, holding the wisdom, clarity, and understanding that lie beyond the ego's limitations. Reaching this level of awareness shifts one's journey, transcending external influences and accessing profound insight that brings comfort and direction. In the connection to the Higher Self, participants access their core truth, an alignment that illuminates their purpose and clarifies the steps toward fulfillment. This chapter explores the foundational practices of accessing the Higher Self, cultivating a dialogue with this inner wisdom.

The journey toward the Higher Self begins with a simple acknowledgment: this connection already exists within each person, waiting to be discovered. The Higher Self is not something outside or distant; it is the intrinsic awareness that exists beyond the conscious mind. To reach this level of awareness, participants are encouraged to let go of self-doubt, worry, and mental noise. Reaching beyond these constraints is a journey of trust, inviting participants to release fears and judgments to glimpse the Higher Self's presence, calm and unyielding, beneath it all.

Meditative practices become essential in this exploration. Meditation quiets the mind, allowing participants to sink below everyday thoughts and mental chatter, connecting to the inner stillness where the Higher Self resides. A simple yet powerful technique is to focus on the breath, following each inhale and exhale, noticing the gradual transition from surface awareness to a deeper inner calm. With practice, participants may begin to feel an expansive presence within this quiet, a sense of being that is free from ego or fear. This state of inner silence is the doorway through which the Higher Self begins to reveal itself.

Visualization further supports this connection. One effective visualization involves imagining a journey to a sacred space within, a place that feels safe, wise, and deeply personal. Participants may imagine walking through a forest, crossing a river, or following a lighted path until they reach this inner sanctuary. In this visualization, they may encounter a figure or light representing their Higher Self, embodying unconditional compassion and wisdom. Here, they may ask questions or simply observe, allowing insights to flow naturally. This practice brings the Higher Self into focus, making it accessible as a guide and source of comfort.

Journaling serves as a bridge between this inner experience and daily life, allowing participants to capture and interpret the messages received during meditation or visualization. Through journaling, they record impressions, symbols, or sensations that arose, reflecting on their meaning and connection to their life. This practice helps integrate the insights from the Higher Self, making them tangible and applicable. Each entry becomes a personal dialogue, a conversation between the conscious mind and the Higher Self that deepens self-understanding and clarity over time.

The presence of the Higher Self is often felt as a calm, intuitive knowing—distinct from mental analysis or external influence. To distinguish this voice from the ego or fear, participants learn to sense the quality of the message itself. Ego-driven thoughts are often urgent or judgmental, while insights from the Higher Self feel clear, gentle, and unwavering. These insights do not push but rather invite, resonating with a sense of peace. This inner knowing guides participants to choices that align with their true values, making life feel purposeful and harmonious. Recognizing the tone of the Higher Self's voice helps participants discern their intuition, building confidence in this connection.

Practices such as gratitude and self-compassion further enhance this relationship. By regularly expressing gratitude and acceptance, participants create an inner atmosphere that aligns with the Higher Self's qualities. Gratitude shifts focus from scarcity to abundance, reinforcing the sense that all experiences contribute to growth and understanding. Self-compassion, in turn, nurtures a supportive inner environment, dissolving self-criticism and replacing it with kindness. This practice mirrors the Higher Self's perspective, embracing one's humanity with acceptance. Through these qualities, participants draw closer to the essence of their Higher Self, resonating with its peaceful and wise nature.

To anchor the insights from the Higher Self in daily life, participants learn to engage in brief moments of mindfulness throughout the day. By pausing to center themselves, they reconnect with the inner stillness cultivated in meditation, aligning with the Higher Self's perspective. These pauses can be as simple as taking a few conscious breaths, observing the surroundings, or recalling the sense of calm from meditation. These moments of mindfulness become touchpoints, gentle reminders of the Higher Self's presence that anchor participants even amid life's challenges.

As participants grow in their connection to the Higher Self, they experience a transformation in how they relate to themselves and others. This connection fosters a state of acceptance and openness, guiding them to view experiences from a place of clarity and compassion. Rather than reacting to life's challenges with fear or resistance, they approach them as opportunities for growth, trusting that the Higher Self provides guidance at every step. This inner alignment transforms their journey, grounding them in their essence, free from the pull of ego-driven fears or doubts.

Connecting with the Higher Self is not a single moment but a continuous unfolding, a practice that deepens with attention and intention. In each quiet meditation, each journaled insight, and each mindful pause, participants return to this essence, discovering a place of wisdom that offers clarity and peace. Through this journey, they realize that the Higher Self is always present, waiting to guide, comfort, and inspire from within. This connection becomes a compass, a source of empowerment and understanding that enriches every aspect of their lives, illuminating a path of authenticity and profound self-discovery.

Having established a connection with the Higher Self, participants now explore practices that deepen this relationship, expanding their access to inner wisdom and intuition. This stage emphasizes techniques that enhance the dialogue with the Higher Self, empowering participants to draw from their inner guidance in moments of decision, healing, and personal growth. Through visualization, guided meditation, and intention-setting, participants strengthen this connection, experiencing a continuous alignment with the wisdom and insight that exists within.

One profound practice for accessing the Higher Self's wisdom is guided visualization. In this advanced technique, participants are guided to imagine themselves standing at the edge of a tranquil place, such as a lake or an open field, where they meet a symbolic representation of their Higher Self. This figure—often seen as a wise guide, light, or compassionate presence—becomes a source of profound insight. In the quiet of this sacred encounter, participants may ask questions or simply listen, receiving impressions, sensations, or symbols that convey the Higher Self's guidance. This practice strengthens trust in the inner voice, transforming abstract intuition into a direct experience of clarity.

Automatic writing is another powerful tool for accessing the Higher Self. Participants enter a meditative state, calming the mind and setting an intention to connect with their inner wisdom. With a journal or paper before them, they begin to write freely, without censoring or editing their thoughts. Often, as the hand moves across the page, words and messages emerge that feel clear, wise, and distinct from ordinary thought patterns. Automatic writing allows participants to bypass the critical mind, opening a channel for the Higher Self's messages to flow. This practice is particularly helpful when clarity is needed around a specific question, as it offers direct insight that can be read and reflected upon over time.

Intention-setting becomes a vital element in maintaining an active connection with the Higher Self. By setting a clear intention to receive guidance, participants signal their readiness to listen and align with this inner wisdom. This intention can be stated aloud or in writing at the beginning of meditation or visualization sessions. For instance, they might affirm, "I am open to the wisdom of my Higher Self and trust in its guidance." Setting this intention reinforces the participant's commitment to their inner journey, creating a focused energy that facilitates the connection. Over time, this practice cultivates a natural habit of turning inward, trusting that the Higher Self is always available for support.

The mirror meditation technique offers a profound way to deepen self-awareness and insight. In this practice, participants sit in front of a mirror and look into their own eyes, quieting their thoughts and focusing on the presence they see before them. They begin to observe the subtle expressions and emotions reflected back, as if looking beyond the physical self into their deeper being. With patience, many experience a shift, sensing the Higher Self looking back with compassion and wisdom. This exercise can be transformative, as it confronts participants with their true essence, helping them to dissolve self-judgment and connect directly with their inner wisdom.

Guided meditation for intuitive enhancement allows participants to fine-tune their natural intuition. During this meditation, participants imagine a golden light filling their mind and heart, enhancing clarity and insight. They may focus on a question or situation, inviting any images, thoughts, or sensations that arise to provide insight. This practice creates a receptive mental space, where intuition is encouraged to surface without interference from doubt or overthinking. Participants often experience subtle impressions, such as colors, feelings, or memories, that provide guidance and understanding. Over time, this practice develops their confidence in intuitive insights as valid expressions of the Higher Self's wisdom.

Dreamwork is another advanced method for connecting with the Higher Self. Before sleep, participants set an intention to receive guidance or insight through their dreams, perhaps focusing on a question or concern. Upon waking, they write down any dreams or impressions, reflecting on the symbols, emotions, or messages that may relate to their intention. Dreams can often serve as powerful communications from the subconscious, where the Higher Self communicates through imagery and metaphor. Interpreting these symbols allows participants to access deeper layers of understanding, often revealing perspectives that the conscious mind may overlook.

To integrate this inner wisdom into daily life, mindful action becomes essential. Mindful action involves approaching each decision, task, or interaction with a conscious awareness of the Higher Self's qualities—compassion, clarity, and authenticity. By practicing mindfulness in everyday choices, participants begin to live in alignment with the guidance they receive. This practice encourages a consistent, lived expression of the Higher Self, where inner wisdom becomes the foundation of all actions, transforming ordinary experiences into opportunities for growth and alignment.

Regular reflection and review further solidify the connection with the Higher Self. Participants are encouraged to set aside time each week to review insights gained, recording any recurring themes, symbols, or messages that have appeared in meditation, writing, or dreams. By reflecting on these insights, participants observe patterns of guidance, reinforcing the presence of the Higher Self's wisdom in their lives. This practice not only deepens trust but also creates a record of personal growth, illuminating the path they have traveled and the transformation they continue to experience.

The relationship with the Higher Self is a lifelong journey, a continuous unfolding of inner wisdom that becomes more profound with each practice and intention. By actively cultivating this connection through visualization, meditation, and mindful living, participants discover an unwavering source of guidance, a wellspring of clarity that illuminates their path forward. In this relationship, they find strength, comfort, and insight that transcend the fluctuations of external life. With each deepening of this connection, participants come to embody the Higher Self more fully, living from a place of wisdom, authenticity, and peace. This inner alignment becomes their foundation, grounding them in a truth that is both timeless and intimately personal.

Chapter 14
Subconscious Memories and Personal Archetypes

Within the subconscious lies a rich tapestry of memories, symbols, and archetypes that shape the mind and influence behavior. Accessing these hidden aspects brings understanding and healing, as participants uncover how past experiences and ingrained archetypes impact their present selves. Subconscious memories—whether from childhood, formative life events, or ancestral roots—leave imprints on the psyche. Personal archetypes, or the symbolic figures that embody core aspects of the self, guide how we see ourselves and respond to the world. In this chapter, we begin exploring techniques to gently retrieve these subconscious elements, illuminating parts of the self that may be ready for recognition and release.

The journey into the subconscious begins with gentle visualization, a safe, guided process that allows participants to access memories or images without force. In this practice, participants are guided to imagine a safe, peaceful setting—a meadow, forest, or sanctuary where they feel secure and open. Within this setting, they are invited to observe any sensations, images, or emotions that surface naturally. This visualization technique allows participants to move beyond conscious memory and access the images held within the subconscious, where memories often emerge in symbolic or metaphorical forms. By allowing these memories to appear gently, participants can begin to explore their significance without feeling overwhelmed.

Introspective meditation offers another pathway into subconscious memories. This meditation begins with focused breathing, which calms the mind and opens a receptive state. Participants may ask themselves, "What memory or experience holds meaning for me now?" They then let their minds flow, observing what surfaces without directing or analyzing. Often, subtle memories or sensations appear, leading participants to a deeper understanding of unprocessed emotions or hidden influences. This practice requires patience and curiosity, as it often takes repeated sessions for subconscious memories to fully reveal themselves. Over time, however, these memories provide valuable insights, offering keys to emotional patterns and responses.

Working with symbols and dreams is another powerful method for exploring subconscious memories. Dreams are rich with imagery and symbols, often conveying messages from the subconscious that the conscious mind may resist or overlook. Participants are encouraged to keep a dream journal, noting symbols, colors, emotions, and recurring themes that emerge. Upon reflection, they may recognize how certain symbols relate to specific life experiences or unresolved memories. By paying attention to these symbols, participants tap into a language that bypasses logic and speaks directly to their inner awareness, revealing layers of meaning and understanding hidden in daily consciousness.

An essential element in this journey is the understanding of archetypes. Archetypes are universal symbols or characters that represent core human experiences, such as the Hero, the Shadow, the Child, or the Caregiver. Each archetype embodies specific qualities and patterns of behavior, and many people find themselves resonating with particular archetypes throughout different phases of life. By recognizing and understanding personal archetypes, participants begin to see how these symbolic figures influence their attitudes, choices, and self-perception. For instance, the Hero archetype may encourage one to be courageous, while the Shadow archetype may reveal hidden fears or unresolved conflicts.

In exploring these archetypes, guided introspection can be useful. Participants might ask, "What archetype do I resonate with at this moment?" or "How does this archetype influence my responses?" By contemplating these questions, they may notice how particular archetypes are present in their daily lives, relationships, or challenges. Recognizing these patterns brings awareness to unconscious motivations, helping participants to interact with these aspects of themselves with greater intention and understanding.

The inner child is one such archetype that often holds deep memories and emotions from early life experiences. This child archetype embodies the essence of innocence, curiosity, and vulnerability. By connecting with the inner child, participants can access childhood memories, both joyful and painful, that continue to shape their perspectives and emotional responses. Techniques such as writing a letter to the inner child or visualizing a supportive interaction with this younger self allow participants to revisit these memories with compassion. This connection often reveals past wounds or unmet needs, offering an opportunity for healing and integration.

To support this exploration, affirmations of safety and self-acceptance create a foundation of trust. Affirmations such as "I am safe to explore my memories," or "I accept all parts of myself with compassion" reinforce the inner environment needed to approach subconscious material without fear. These affirmations encourage participants to view memories and archetypes not as burdens but as parts of themselves that offer wisdom and insight. With this acceptance, participants build the resilience needed to work with their subconscious without feeling vulnerable or threatened.

Working with the subconscious also requires a strong sense of grounding. Techniques such as deep breathing, body awareness, and grounding exercises ensure that participants remain present, even when accessing intense or emotionally charged memories. Grounding practices anchor them in the present moment, creating a sense of stability and control that enables them to explore deeper layers without feeling overwhelmed. With grounding, participants can journey through their subconscious with clarity, observing rather than reacting, allowing insights to emerge naturally.

Reflective journaling supports this process by capturing the symbols, memories, and insights that arise. Through journaling, participants document their inner discoveries, describing the images, emotions, or archetypes that appeared in meditation or dreams. Reflecting on these entries over time helps to reveal patterns, connections, and recurring themes, reinforcing the journey of self-discovery. Journaling not only preserves these insights but also serves as a mirror, allowing participants to see their growth, shifts in perspective, and the unfolding of a deeper self-awareness.

Exploring subconscious memories and personal archetypes is a path to understanding and embracing the fullness of one's inner world. By acknowledging these hidden aspects, participants learn to integrate their experiences, releasing old patterns and creating space for authenticity and freedom. This journey into the subconscious is not only a journey of remembering but of reuniting with the true self, as each memory, symbol, and archetype offers another step toward inner wholeness.

Building on the initial exploration of subconscious memories and personal archetypes, participants now deepen their practice, using advanced techniques to access, reinterpret, and integrate these aspects of their inner world. This stage of work transforms insights into healing as participants revisit their subconscious memories with compassion and explore archetypal influences more consciously. By engaging in practices that safely allow memories and archetypes to surface, participants move toward wholeness, bridging past experiences with present awareness.

Regression meditation is a powerful tool for revisiting formative memories. In this practice, participants enter a deep, relaxed state, guided gently toward an earlier time in their life or a specific memory that holds emotional or psychological weight. Rather than simply reliving the memory, participants are encouraged to observe it from a detached perspective, like an onlooker viewing a scene. This approach allows them to witness the memory without becoming overwhelmed by the emotions tied to it. By returning to these moments with a sense of calm and distance, participants gain a clearer understanding of how these past events influenced their beliefs, emotional responses, and behaviors. Often, seeing the memory from this perspective brings new insights that were not accessible before, offering a fresh understanding of the self.

In cases where memories carry strong emotions, inner dialogue techniques provide a way to release and transform these feelings. Participants engage in a dialogue between their current self and the part of themselves that experienced the memory. This may involve visualizing a conversation with a younger self, offering reassurance, understanding, or forgiveness. This compassionate interaction helps to heal old wounds, allowing past pain to be acknowledged and resolved. For instance, participants might imagine themselves comforting their inner child during a moment of past sadness or fear, providing the support they needed but may not have received at the time. Through this practice, the emotional charge around the memory often dissipates, transforming it from a source of pain into one of acceptance and peace.

As participants revisit memories, they also work with the Shadow archetype, representing the hidden or repressed parts of the self. The Shadow often contains aspects of the personality that were deemed unacceptable or unwanted, such as anger, fear, or vulnerability. Through Shadow work, participants explore these parts not as faults, but as aspects of themselves that require understanding and integration. Techniques such as journaling or visualizing interactions with the Shadow help participants see these traits as parts of the human experience, allowing them to embrace a more complete version of themselves. This process releases the Shadow's influence over behavior and decision-making, as these traits are acknowledged rather than suppressed.

Another powerful technique is symbolic art expression, where participants use drawing, painting, or other forms of creativity to represent subconscious memories or archetypes. This art practice bypasses the analytical mind, allowing emotions and images from the subconscious to emerge freely. Participants may create visual representations of memories, archetypes, or emotions without needing to understand them fully. For example, drawing the Child, Hero, or Shadow archetype might reveal insights that words cannot capture. Through colors, shapes, and forms, participants express what lies within, seeing patterns or emotions that were previously hidden. Symbolic art becomes a means of dialogue with the subconscious, bringing clarity and integration through creative expression.

In working with personal archetypes, archetypal role-play provides a way to actively embody these inner symbols. Participants choose an archetype that resonates, whether it be the Warrior, the Healer, or the Seeker, and act out this role in a safe setting. They might explore how this archetype moves, speaks, and interacts, noticing any emotions or insights that arise. By embodying the archetype, participants experience it as part of themselves, gaining a sense of empowerment and familiarity with these symbolic aspects. Role-play helps dissolve the boundaries between conscious and subconscious, integrating the archetype into the self and allowing participants to carry its strengths into their lives.

In ritual closure practices, participants honor the memories and archetypes that surfaced, symbolically releasing or integrating them. For instance, they might write down insights or emotions on paper and then burn or bury it as a gesture of release. Alternatively, they may place a symbol of the archetype on an altar or in a special space to honor its presence and influence. Ritual closure provides a sense of completion, marking the work done with reverence. These rituals allow participants to let go of past burdens, solidifying their journey and preparing them to move forward.

Affirmations for integration reinforce the acceptance of all parts of the self. By affirming, "I honor all parts of my experience," or "I am whole and complete," participants embody the understanding that each memory and archetype contributes to their unique identity. These affirmations anchor their journey into daily life, transforming the way they relate to themselves. Each affirmation becomes a reminder that past wounds and hidden aspects have value, helping participants to maintain the healing and insights gained.

As they complete this deeper exploration, participants engage in weekly reflection and journaling, tracking the shifts they observe in thoughts, emotions, and self-perception. This reflective practice helps them document progress, noticing how the integration of memories and archetypes influences their choices and relationships. By observing these changes, participants gain confidence in their journey, seeing tangible signs of transformation and growth.

Through these practices, participants release what no longer serves them and embrace what has been hidden, creating a balance between conscious and subconscious. This advanced work with subconscious memories and archetypes offers not only healing but also a profound sense of wholeness. By integrating these parts of themselves, participants step forward with a greater understanding of who they are, free from the limitations of past conditioning. The journey through the subconscious becomes a journey of empowerment, allowing them to live with authenticity, strength, and inner harmony.

Chapter 15
Energy Purification and Cleansing

Energy purification and cleansing are foundational practices within liberation and rebirth therapy, helping to clear emotional residue and stagnant energy that accumulate over time. As participants journey inward, these cleansing rituals provide a renewed sense of vitality, clarity, and openness, creating an energetic environment that supports their path of healing. This chapter introduces core techniques that work with natural elements—water, fire, air, and earth—to purify and balance the energy body. Each element brings a unique quality to the cleansing process, encouraging a release of blockages and a restoration of harmonious flow.

Water is the first and perhaps the most familiar element in energy purification. Water carries a natural cleansing quality, symbolizing flow, surrender, and emotional release. Participants can work with water in a variety of ways, from taking intentional baths or showers to practicing water meditation. In a cleansing bath ritual, for instance, participants may add sea salt, essential oils, or herbs like lavender or rosemary, each chosen for their purifying properties. As they submerge, they are encouraged to visualize the water drawing out negativity or unwanted energy, washing it away. Through this ritual, water serves as both a physical and symbolic purifier, allowing participants to feel refreshed, calm, and energetically renewed.

Fire, in contrast, represents transformation, courage, and the power to transmute energy. The energy of fire encourages the release of fears, limiting beliefs, and emotions that may feel heavy or burdensome. One common practice for working with fire is the burning ceremony, where participants write down thoughts, patterns, or experiences they wish to release on a small piece of paper, then set it aflame in a safe space. As the paper burns, they visualize these aspects dissolving, freeing them from what no longer serves. The warmth and light of the flame bring a sense of clarity and empowerment, transforming old energy into something lighter and more vibrant. This ritual connects participants with their inner strength, symbolizing their readiness to let go and embrace transformation.

The element of air brings the qualities of lightness, clarity, and movement, supporting participants in clearing mental or emotional fog. Breathing exercises, wind cleansing rituals, and working with incense or smudging are all ways to harness the purifying energy of air. Smudging, in particular, involves burning sacred herbs—such as sage, cedar, or palo santo—and waving the smoke around the body or space. This practice is both grounding and cleansing, dispersing stagnant energy and inviting clarity. Participants might use a feather to guide the smoke, allowing it to gently encircle their aura, clearing out thoughts or emotions that feel heavy or stagnant. The air ritual aligns participants with clarity, focus, and an openness to new perspectives, helping them feel mentally refreshed and energetically lightened.

Earth, as the fourth element, offers grounding and stability, providing a foundation for cleansing rituals that restore balance. Earth-based practices often involve physical connection with the ground, such as walking barefoot on natural soil, touching trees, or burying stones with intentions in the earth. One effective method for earth cleansing is the salt bowl ritual, where participants place a bowl of salt in a room or near themselves while meditating. Salt naturally absorbs and neutralizes negative energy, so placing intentions into the salt helps to pull unwanted energies from the body or space. Afterward, the salt is discarded or returned to the earth, carrying the purified energy with it. Earth rituals create a sense of grounding and inner stability, reinforcing the participant's connection to their body, nature, and the present moment.

These element-based cleansing practices work on both an energetic and symbolic level, inviting participants to actively participate in their own purification. Each element holds a unique power, and as participants choose and combine these methods, they create a personalized cleansing experience that resonates with their specific needs. Over time, these practices become a valuable part of their spiritual and therapeutic routines, tools that maintain energetic clarity and balance as they move through their journey.

Participants may also incorporate mantras or affirmations during these cleansing rituals to reinforce their intentions. Mantras such as "I release all that no longer serves me" or "I am purified, renewed, and aligned with my highest self" echo the energy-clearing process, aligning thoughts and intentions with the physical and energetic act of purification. Repeating these affirmations helps participants stay focused and grounded in their intention, amplifying the cleansing effects and bringing their entire being into alignment with the ritual.

Another supportive practice is energetic visualization, where participants imagine a white or golden light moving through their body, clearing out any dark or stagnant areas. This light represents pure energy, gently moving from head to toe, illuminating and releasing all that no longer serves. As the light moves, participants might feel tension dissolve, replaced by a sensation of openness or lightness. Visualization strengthens the participant's connection with their inner energy, creating a powerful internal cleansing that complements physical rituals. This practice can be done on its own or combined with any of the elemental methods for a layered, holistic approach to energy purification.

Grounding exercises are essential following any energy cleansing ritual, as they help participants integrate the renewed energy into their physical body and environment. Techniques such as visualizing roots extending from the feet into the earth, focusing on steady breathing, or simply placing one's hands on the ground help participants feel stable and connected. Grounding reinforces the cleansing effects, ensuring that the energy released does not linger and that the participant feels centered and present.

Through these practices, energy purification becomes a powerful tool for clearing, revitalizing, and aligning the self. The regular use of elemental cleansing not only clears the participant's energy field but also enhances their resilience, intuition, and inner peace. These rituals build a foundation of energetic clarity, creating an environment in which participants can continue their journey of liberation and rebirth with an open heart and renewed spirit. The process of cleansing aligns the mind, body, and spirit, grounding the participant in a state of balance that prepares them for deeper healing and transformation.

Having introduced the foundational practices of energy purification, this chapter delves into advanced techniques that work with energetic tools, visualization, and sound to deepen the cleansing process. These methods encourage participants to release subtle, deeply ingrained energy patterns, creating space for greater harmony and clarity in the mind, body, and spirit. By working with tools like crystals, sound frequencies, and energy-based visualizations, participants further develop their ability to clear stagnant energy, inviting profound renewal and transformation into their lives.

Crystal cleansing offers a powerful way to purify and enhance energy fields. Crystals such as clear quartz, amethyst, black tourmaline, and selenite have been used for centuries for their ability to absorb, amplify, and balance energies. To use crystals in purification, participants select stones based on their properties—black tourmaline for protection, amethyst for emotional clarity, or selenite for energetic cleansing. Participants can hold these crystals while meditating, place them on areas of the body where energy feels blocked, or arrange them around their space to maintain a balanced environment. Crystals serve as both amplifiers and stabilizers, harmonizing the energy field and promoting a sense of calm and renewal. When using crystals for cleansing, participants are encouraged to periodically cleanse the crystals themselves, either by rinsing them with water (for water-safe crystals), placing them in sunlight or moonlight, or using incense to refresh their energy.

Sound cleansing harnesses the power of vibrational frequency to dislodge and dissolve stagnant energy. Sound tools such as singing bowls, tuning forks, and bells resonate at frequencies that penetrate and purify the energetic body, breaking up dense or stuck energies. Participants can begin by gently striking a singing bowl or ringing a bell around themselves or within a room, allowing the sound waves to move through their space. As the sound vibrates, it clears away residual energy, inviting an atmosphere of harmony and lightness. Participants may also experiment with chanting or toning sounds, such as "OM," to create resonance within the body, which encourages alignment and balance. Each sound connects with different frequencies within the body, so participants are invited to explore and discover which resonates most deeply with their unique energy field.

Breath-based visualization is an advanced technique that uses the power of the breath to cleanse the body's energy centers, or chakras. Participants visualize each inhale drawing in pure, cleansing energy, and each exhale releasing any stagnant or heavy energy. They may begin at the base of the spine, focusing on each chakra as they move up the body with each breath, imagining a radiant light clearing and aligning each energy center. By visualizing the breath as a flow of pure light, participants experience a full energetic reset, helping each chakra return to its natural state of openness and harmony. This breathwork practice builds awareness and sensitivity to the energy body, fostering a deep and lasting sense of energetic balance.

Color visualization further supports energy cleansing, using the power of color to restore harmony to the energy field. Participants may visualize surrounding themselves with a specific color based on the desired effect: white for purity, blue for calm, green for healing, or gold for spiritual alignment. In this practice, they imagine breathing in the chosen color and allowing it to fill every part of their body and aura. This infusion of color purifies and revitalizes their energy, helping to clear out any energetic disruptions and bring in a sense of peace. Color visualization can be tailored to specific intentions, adding depth to other cleansing practices by connecting with the energetic frequencies associated with each color.

To sustain this purified state, participants can incorporate energy protection visualizations, ensuring that they remain energetically balanced as they move through daily life. One popular method is the protective bubble visualization, where participants imagine a sphere of light surrounding their body, shielding them from external negativity while allowing positive energy to flow freely. This sphere acts as a buffer, helping to maintain the benefits of the cleansing practices even in challenging environments. Participants may reinforce this visualization by choosing a color for the protective sphere, such as violet for spiritual protection or blue for calmness and clarity. By reinforcing this boundary, participants remain energetically centered, feeling both safe and connected to their inner clarity.

Working with intentional movement, such as tai chi, qi gong, or yoga, also serves as a dynamic form of energy purification. Each movement in these practices is designed to encourage a balanced flow of energy, gently releasing blocks and promoting alignment throughout the body. Participants can choose a series of gentle, flowing movements that encourage relaxation and flow, visualizing energy moving freely through their entire being. Intentional movement not only cleanses but also strengthens the energy body, helping participants feel grounded and fully present. Over time, these practices build resilience, making it easier to release energy blockages and maintain an open, fluid energy field.

As participants deepen their practice, mantras for ongoing purification provide a supportive foundation. Repeating mantras such as "I am clear, I am balanced, I am aligned," or "My energy is pure and harmonious," reinforces their intention for continued energy clarity. Participants may use these mantras during meditation, breathwork, or movement practices to enhance the cleansing effect, aligning their thoughts and emotions with the energy work they are doing. These affirmations help them stay focused on their journey of purification, acting as reminders of the clarity and balance they cultivate through these advanced practices.

To conclude each cleansing ritual, participants can perform a simple grounding exercise to integrate the purified energy into their physical and emotional bodies. Placing their hands on the earth or imagining roots extending from their feet into the ground, they connect deeply with the stability of the earth, anchoring the effects of the ritual. This grounding process ensures that the shifts made in the energy body are harmoniously incorporated, allowing participants to move forward feeling centered and revitalized.

Through these advanced practices of energy purification, participants are empowered to cleanse and strengthen their energy field, cultivating resilience, clarity, and inner harmony. Working with crystals, sound, color, breath, and protective visualizations, they deepen their connection to their own energy, enhancing their sense of presence and peace. Over time, these techniques become a source of renewal and balance, supporting participants as they progress on their path of liberation and rebirth. As they integrate these practices into daily life, they experience a transformation not only in their energy but also in their entire being, embodying the clarity and lightness that energy purification brings.

Chapter 16
Chakras and Energy Centers

The chakras, or energy centers, form a core foundation for understanding the energy body in liberation and rebirth therapy. These centers, often depicted as spinning wheels of energy along the spine, are believed to influence our emotional, mental, and spiritual states. Each chakra is connected to different aspects of our well-being, shaping how we process experiences, hold beliefs, and express ourselves. By working with chakras, participants can recognize where imbalances or blockages lie, allowing them to restore balance and strengthen their energy flow, a vital step for profound transformation and healing.

The journey through the chakras begins at the Root Chakra (Muladhara), located at the base of the spine. This chakra is connected to survival instincts, security, and physical vitality. When balanced, the Root Chakra offers a sense of stability and grounding, creating a solid foundation for growth. If this chakra is blocked, participants may feel anxious, insecure, or disconnected. Root Chakra work often includes grounding exercises, mindful walking, or connecting with the earth. Visualizing a deep red color in this area or repeating affirmations like "I am safe, I am grounded" helps activate and stabilize this energy center, reinforcing a sense of connection to the physical world.

Moving upward, the Sacral Chakra (Svadhisthana) is located just below the navel and governs emotions, pleasure, and creativity. The Sacral Chakra is associated with the flow of emotions and the capacity for joy. A balanced Sacral Chakra allows for healthy emotional expression and a connection to pleasure and creativity. If blocked, it may lead to emotional suppression or lack of inspiration. Meditation focused on the color orange and gentle, flowing movements like dance are effective ways to balance this chakra. Affirmations like "I embrace change and creativity" can further enhance its energy, helping participants feel free and expressive.

The Solar Plexus Chakra (Manipura), located in the upper abdomen, is the center of self-confidence, personal power, and will. When balanced, the Solar Plexus Chakra empowers one's sense of purpose and determination. A blockage here may manifest as low self-esteem, indecisiveness, or a feeling of powerlessness. To activate this energy center, participants can visualize a warm, golden light radiating from the abdomen, symbolizing strength and clarity. Practicing assertiveness and setting boundaries can further support this chakra, promoting a healthy sense of identity and self-worth. Affirmations such as "I am strong, I am confident" reinforce its energy.

The Heart Chakra (Anahata), located at the center of the chest, is connected to love, compassion, and emotional balance. It serves as the bridge between the lower, physical chakras and the higher, spiritual ones. When open, the Heart Chakra allows for empathy, compassion, and a sense of interconnectedness with others. A blocked Heart Chakra can lead to feelings of isolation, jealousy, or a struggle to forgive. Meditating on the color green or pink and practicing acts of kindness can help open this chakra. Affirmations like "I give and receive love freely" encourage its balance, fostering a spirit of acceptance and compassion.

Above the heart is the Throat Chakra (Vishuddha), situated at the throat, governing communication, self-expression, and truth. A balanced Throat Chakra supports clear and authentic communication, both with others and oneself. Blockages here can lead to difficulty expressing thoughts or emotions, or even a fear of speaking one's truth. Visualizing a bright blue light around the throat area, practicing speaking affirmations, or engaging in journaling can help unblock this chakra. Statements like "I speak my truth openly and with confidence" activate this center, promoting honest and respectful self-expression.

The Third Eye Chakra (Ajna), located between the eyebrows, is associated with intuition, perception, and inner wisdom. This chakra is the gateway to the inner self, guiding insight and clarity beyond ordinary perception. When balanced, the Third Eye Chakra enhances intuition and the ability to see beyond surface realities. Blockages may result in confusion, lack of foresight, or a disconnection from inner guidance. Meditation focusing on an indigo or deep violet light at the third eye, along with practices that cultivate mindfulness and self-reflection, stimulate this chakra. Affirmations like "I trust my intuition" enhance clarity, allowing for deeper self-understanding.

At the crown of the head lies the Crown Chakra (Sahasrara), the center of spirituality and connection to universal consciousness. The Crown Chakra represents our connection to the divine, unity, and transcendence. When balanced, it brings a sense of peace, clarity, and connection to something greater than oneself. A blocked Crown Chakra may lead to feelings of disconnection, closed-mindedness, or a sense of purposelessness. Meditation on a violet or white light at the crown, visualizing an opening to universal energy, helps activate this chakra. Affirmations such as "I am connected to universal wisdom" can nurture a sense of unity and transcendence, deepening spiritual awareness.

Working through these chakras creates an awareness of how energy flows through the body and mind, helping participants identify areas that need healing or strengthening. For each chakra, participants may keep a journal, noting sensations, emotions, or memories that arise when focusing on that specific center. This practice allows for a holistic view of the energy body, identifying where imbalances might stem from past experiences or beliefs that need to be released or rebalanced.

Through this foundational work, participants begin to understand the unique role each chakra plays in their overall well-being, paving the way for further practices that enhance energy alignment. The exploration of each chakra becomes a journey of self-discovery, connecting body, mind, and spirit in a harmonious flow that supports their healing and rebirth. As participants continue, this awareness of the chakras fosters a relationship with their inner energy, opening the path toward more profound levels of transformation and self-understanding.

With a foundational understanding of the chakras, participants can now deepen their exploration by learning specific techniques to unlock, align, and energize each energy center. These practices enhance the harmonious flow of energy through the body, essential for personal healing and spiritual growth. By actively working to balance the chakras, participants not only cleanse stagnant energy but also experience heightened awareness, resilience, and alignment with their true selves.

One of the most effective methods for chakra activation is focused breathing. Each chakra can be nurtured through directed breathwork, helping participants clear and empower each center individually. Beginning with the Root Chakra, participants breathe deeply into the area, visualizing the breath as a vibrant red light expanding and filling this base energy center. Each breath invites strength and grounding. Moving up through each chakra, participants change the color and intention of their breath to match the chakra's energy, gradually reaching the Crown Chakra, where they visualize the breath as a radiant white or violet light, expanding their consciousness. This guided journey through the chakras, known as chakra breathing meditation, is a powerful tool for achieving full energetic alignment and for grounding their awareness in each energy center.

Sound therapy also supports chakra activation, using vibrations to resonate with each chakra's unique frequency. Each chakra is associated with a specific sound or mantra, such as "LAM" for the Root Chakra, "VAM" for the Sacral Chakra, and so forth. Chanting these sounds or playing tuning forks at each chakra's frequency helps clear blockages, inviting clarity and alignment. Participants may chant these sounds aloud, allowing the vibrations to resonate within the body, or play the tones in their environment while meditating on each chakra. This process not only harmonizes each energy center but also enhances the participant's intuitive sensitivity to the chakras, creating a direct experience of how sound interacts with their energy.

Crystal placement offers another approach to chakra alignment, using the unique properties of crystals to clear and balance energy. By placing specific crystals on each chakra during meditation, participants can amplify the natural qualities of each center. Red jasper or black tourmaline, for instance, strengthens grounding at the Root Chakra, while rose quartz encourages love and compassion at the Heart Chakra. For the Third Eye, amethyst supports intuition, while clear quartz at the Crown Chakra enhances spiritual connection. Participants may also meditate while holding a chosen crystal, allowing its energy to harmonize and amplify the corresponding chakra. This technique is especially powerful when combined with visualization or affirmations, as the crystals act as conduits for focused intention, deepening the energetic effects.

Guided visualization brings a unique depth to chakra work by immersing participants in the healing imagery of each chakra. For instance, while focusing on the Solar Plexus Chakra, participants might imagine a bright, radiant sun centered in their abdomen, empowering their will and vitality. As they move to the Heart Chakra, they envision a lush green landscape, symbolizing growth, balance, and love. Visualization creates a bridge between the mind and energy body, helping participants bring conscious intention to each chakra. By visualizing colors, shapes, or scenes that represent harmony and strength, participants stimulate healing and balance in each energy center, allowing them to experience the chakras as vibrant, dynamic forces within themselves.

Mudras and physical postures provide an embodied approach to chakra alignment. Each chakra corresponds to certain mudras, or hand gestures, and yoga poses that help activate and balance its energy. For example, the Root Chakra connects to grounding poses like Mountain Pose or Warrior, which foster stability and connection to the earth. Heart-opening postures, such as Camel Pose, stimulate the Heart Chakra, encouraging openness and emotional release. Participants can enhance these postures with specific mudras, such as Anjali Mudra (prayer position) for the Heart Chakra or Gyan Mudra (thumb and index finger together) for the Crown Chakra, which amplify energy flow. Practicing these postures and mudras regularly builds a deeper connection to each chakra, fostering alignment between the physical body and the energy centers.

Affirmations for each chakra play a significant role in reinforcing positive energy within each center. As participants meditate or breathe into a chakra, they can repeat affirmations aligned with that chakra's qualities. For the Root Chakra, "I am grounded and secure"; for the Sacral Chakra, "I embrace my emotions and creativity"; for the Solar Plexus Chakra, "I am strong and confident." These affirmations guide the mind into alignment with the energy body, reinforcing the qualities that each chakra brings. Repeating these affirmations regularly reprograms the subconscious mind, releasing limiting beliefs and replacing them with empowering perspectives.

Energy scanning is an intuitive practice that allows participants to sense and interact with their own energy field. Sitting quietly, they begin by bringing awareness to the space around each chakra, moving their hand slowly over each center to feel any warmth, tingling, or subtle shifts. This exercise cultivates sensitivity to the energy field and helps participants identify which chakras feel balanced or which may need additional focus. As they develop this skill, participants may begin to perceive energy patterns, gaining insight into the underlying causes of any blockages. Energy scanning not only provides valuable feedback but also strengthens the participant's ability to work with their energy intuitively.

Incorporating these advanced techniques into their daily routine, participants build a steady practice of chakra alignment that supports emotional and spiritual resilience. Each technique reinforces the chakras' natural state of harmony, helping participants connect deeply with their inner self and surroundings. As they continue this work, participants often notice shifts in their sense of balance, clarity, and confidence, experiencing the chakras not as abstract concepts but as tangible sources of personal empowerment.

Participants are encouraged to document their chakra experiences in a journal, noting any sensations, emotions, or insights that arise during their practices. By tracking these reflections over time, they build a personal map of their energetic landscape, observing patterns and growth as they progress. These entries become a record of their inner journey, illuminating the shifts and breakthroughs achieved through chakra work.

Through these practices, participants cultivate a relationship with their chakras that is both empowering and healing, creating an inner environment that nurtures continued growth. As each chakra is activated and aligned, participants feel the integration of mind, body, and spirit, connecting to the flow of life with a sense of purpose and openness. This alignment becomes a foundation for all aspects of their journey, empowering them to move forward with renewed strength, insight, and self-awareness.

Chapter 17
Other Rebirth Rituals

With a strong foundation in energy alignment and purification, participants are now ready to explore advanced rebirth rituals that bring new dimensions to their journey. In this next phase, rebirth rituals are revisited with deeper layers of self-understanding and specific intentions, inviting practitioners to transcend their inner limitations and connect more fully with their evolving sense of self. These practices encourage a transformative rebirth, symbolizing the shedding of old beliefs, fears, and attachments that no longer serve, while welcoming an expanded, revitalized self.

At the heart of these rituals is the practice of intentional reflection, where participants revisit core aspects of their identity, habits, and beliefs, preparing for transformation. In a quiet setting, they reflect on questions like, "What parts of my past self am I ready to release?" or "What qualities or intentions do I wish to embody moving forward?" This reflective process sets the stage for the rebirth ritual, clarifying the personal shifts they seek. By bringing conscious awareness to these areas, participants gain a clear sense of purpose for their ritual, knowing what they seek to release and what they wish to manifest in their rebirth.

Symbolic immersion is a profound ritual that marks the transition from the old self to the new. Water is often used for this purpose due to its cleansing and renewing qualities. Participants may choose a body of water, a symbolic bowl, or a shower as their immersive element. In this ritual, they step into the water, visualizing it washing away any outdated beliefs, fears, or emotional burdens that they are ready to leave behind. As they immerse themselves, they visualize emerging renewed, carrying only the qualities and intentions they wish to bring forward. This simple but powerful ritual acts as a symbolic "rebirth," where participants emerge as a new version of themselves, freed from past limitations.

For those seeking a ritual that embraces connection with the earth, grounding rebirth ceremonies are ideal. Participants begin by choosing a natural setting—a forest, field, or garden—where they feel a sense of peace and grounding. Here, they spend time barefoot, placing their hands on the earth, feeling the stability and support of the natural world beneath them. As they breathe deeply, they may state their intentions, visualizing their old self releasing into the earth and their new intentions taking root. This ritual serves as a reminder of the interconnectedness with nature and offers grounding support for the transformation process, aligning participants with the stability of the earth and reinforcing their commitment to growth and renewal.

The fire ritual is an advanced rebirth practice that harnesses the transformative energy of fire to release attachments and limitations. In a safe and prepared environment, participants write down beliefs, patterns, or emotions they wish to release on pieces of paper. As each piece of paper is placed into the flame, they visualize that aspect dissolving, carried away by the smoke. The fire becomes a symbol of courage and transformation, allowing them to witness a visible release of the old self. Participants may then take time to meditate on the energy of the flame, feeling its warmth and embracing the sense of empowerment it brings. This ritual represents a powerful commitment to personal evolution, as participants transform what no longer serves them into fuel for their renewed purpose.

For those seeking to work with the element of air, breath-based rebirth rituals provide a profound experience of letting go and renewal. Participants find a quiet space where they can focus solely on their breathing, beginning with deep, rhythmic breaths. With each exhale, they visualize releasing old energies and attachments, while each inhale fills them with fresh, vibrant energy. As the breathing deepens, participants may experience a natural shift in consciousness, feeling lighter, open, and renewed. This breath-based ritual symbolizes the continuous cycle of release and renewal, encouraging participants to experience rebirth on a cellular level, clearing their energy and allowing them to connect with their inner self.

Guided rebirth meditation offers an inner journey for participants who wish to experience rebirth within a meditative setting. In this meditation, they are guided to envision themselves moving through a symbolic path—perhaps a tunnel, a forest, or a stream—that represents the transition from their old self to their new self. Along the way, they may encounter symbols or figures that offer insights or guidance, helping them reflect on their transformation. As they reach the end of this path, they step into an imagined space of light, feeling the presence of their new self, free from past burdens and limitations. This meditative journey offers a safe, profound experience of rebirth that can be deeply impactful, allowing participants to feel the symbolic shedding of the old self and the welcoming of a fresh perspective.

After any rebirth ritual, participants may complete the experience with intentional grounding, ensuring that their transformation is integrated and sustained. This grounding can take the form of simple breathing, holding a grounding crystal, or spending time in nature to connect with the earth. They may also affirm their intentions aloud, such as "I am renewed, aligned, and open to my highest path," reinforcing the transformation. Grounding after the ritual helps solidify the changes, allowing participants to move forward in life with stability, purpose, and a fresh sense of self-awareness.

Documenting the experience through journaling is highly beneficial, capturing the insights, emotions, and sensations felt during the ritual. Writing about the experience serves as a personal record, offering a space to reflect on what was released and what emerged in its place. Over time, these entries become a testament to their growth and transformation, allowing participants to look back and see how their journey has evolved.

These rebirth rituals are designed to support a profound renewal, empowering participants to step into a higher version of themselves. Each ritual invites them to consciously release old energies and embrace new perspectives, grounding them in the here and now with clarity and strength. Through these practices, rebirth becomes not just a symbolic act but a lived experience, creating a transformative shift that influences all aspects of their lives. With each ritual, participants move closer to embodying their true selves, ready to engage with life from a place of authenticity and inner freedom.

Building on the foundation of rebirth rituals, this chapter introduces deeper practices that allow participants to fully embody their new selves, exploring rituals that encourage them to engage with hidden aspects of their consciousness, strengthen their sense of purpose, and cultivate self-compassion as they release the past. These advanced techniques expand upon the symbolic acts of release, offering participants tools to explore self-rebirth on a profound level that connects mind, body, and spirit.

One of the most potent tools for advanced rebirth is the mirror ritual. This ritual involves standing in front of a mirror and making eye contact with one's reflection while speaking intentions and affirmations aloud. This practice fosters a powerful connection with the self, where participants confront past and present aspects of their identity. Participants begin by acknowledging what they have released—old fears, self-doubts, or outdated beliefs—speaking to themselves with compassion and respect. Then, as they gaze into their own eyes, they declare their new intentions and affirmations, stating qualities they wish to embody, such as "I am free," "I am strong," or "I am worthy of my highest self." The mirror ritual offers a chance to witness the self as both the individual in transition and the reborn being. By engaging with their own reflection, participants allow these affirmations to anchor within, feeling the resonance of their intentions take root.

The creation of a personal rebirth symbol is another technique that empowers participants to connect deeply with their journey. This process begins with introspection, where participants meditate on a symbol, word, or image that represents their rebirth. This symbol might emerge intuitively—a phoenix for transformation, a circle for unity, or a unique design that holds personal meaning. Once the symbol is chosen, participants incorporate it into a physical form, such as drawing it, carving it into wood, or crafting a small piece of jewelry. This symbol becomes a tangible reminder of their rebirth, something they can carry or display to reaffirm their journey and intentions. Every time they interact with the symbol, it serves as an anchor for their renewed self, helping them reconnect with the energy of transformation and rebirth.

An immersive ritual known as the ritual of silence and solitude offers a way to connect with the essence of the rebirth process on an introspective level. Participants set aside a day or a significant period to spend in silence, often in nature or a quiet environment where they can be undisturbed. During this time, they refrain from speaking, using this period to reflect inwardly on the changes they are embracing. Silence allows participants to connect deeply with their inner voice, free from outside influence. Through this practice, they listen to their intuition, observing thoughts, emotions, and intentions as they surface. This ritual often brings clarity and a sense of peace, helping participants feel aligned with their reborn self as they move forward. Solitude becomes a sanctuary, allowing them to recognize and honor their own voice and truth.

The labyrinth walk is another symbolic ritual that represents the journey of rebirth. Participants seek out a physical labyrinth or create one using stones, plants, or markings on the ground. As they walk slowly along the labyrinth's path, they reflect on each phase of their personal journey, allowing memories or past versions of themselves to rise and be released with each step. When they reach the labyrinth's center, participants may meditate or silently affirm their intentions, honoring this space as a symbolic "center" of their reborn self. The walk back out of the labyrinth symbolizes the journey forward, carrying with them the insights and intentions they have gathered. This ritual is powerful for visualizing rebirth as a journey, showing participants how far they've come and encouraging them to embrace the path that lies ahead.

Rebirth through creative expression is a method that channels inner transformation into art, music, dance, or writing. Participants may create a piece of art, compose a song, or write a story that symbolizes their rebirth experience, using their creative expression to convey the emotions, insights, and intentions they carry forward. For instance, painting a landscape or creating a vision board that represents their renewed self provides a visual affirmation of their rebirth. Dance or movement can embody the feeling of shedding the past and stepping into new energy, while writing a poem or narrative can capture the themes of release and transformation in words. This creative ritual makes the rebirth process tangible, celebrating the unique journey each participant has undertaken and solidifying their intentions in a way that feels both personal and liberating.

A more spiritually focused ritual, the rebirth meditation with light, connects participants with the healing energy of light, symbolizing renewal and higher guidance. Participants begin by sitting comfortably, breathing deeply, and visualizing a warm, radiant light above them. As they breathe, they imagine this light gently descending, enveloping them in warmth and purity. The light moves through each part of the body, releasing any remnants of past limitations, and filling each cell with vitality and purpose. As the light reaches their core, participants may state their new intentions, asking for clarity, strength, or wisdom in embodying their reborn self. This meditation aligns participants with a sense of divine guidance, supporting them as they step forward renewed and strengthened in their sense of purpose.

The ritual of release and gratitude is a final, integrative practice that concludes the rebirth journey with an expression of gratitude for the experiences, people, and lessons that have contributed to personal growth. Participants may write down the names of people, memories, or past events on pieces of paper, offering a moment of gratitude for each one before symbolically releasing it. They may burn the papers in a fire, place them in water, or bury them in the earth as a gesture of release. In expressing gratitude, participants honor the past without attachment, recognizing its role in shaping who they have become while affirming their commitment to move forward. This closing ritual brings closure to the rebirth journey, allowing participants to release fully with peace and gratitude.

Journaling after each ritual provides an opportunity to document and process the experience, capturing insights, emotions, and reflections that arise. Participants may note the sensations they felt, any unexpected thoughts, or moments of clarity that emerged, allowing these records to serve as a testament to their growth. Reviewing these entries over time deepens self-understanding and strengthens their commitment to embodying the qualities they have embraced in rebirth.

Each of these advanced rebirth rituals fosters a transformative space, guiding participants through a profound process of release and renewal. They encourage participants to move beyond past limitations, emerging with a clear sense of purpose, resilience, and authenticity. In embracing this deeper phase of rebirth, participants step forward fully empowered, ready to live as their most aligned, liberated selves. This journey of rebirth becomes not merely an event but an ongoing way of living, grounding them in inner strength and guiding them as they navigate the evolving path of self-discovery and spiritual fulfillment.

Chapter 18
Dreams and Symbolism

Dreams and symbols serve as gateways to the subconscious, revealing layers of insight that are often obscured in waking life. Through dreams, participants access hidden aspects of themselves, gaining clues about their emotions, desires, and unresolved experiences. Symbolism, as it appears in both dreams and waking life, acts as a language of the soul, guiding participants through a transformative inner journey. In this chapter, participants are introduced to the fundamentals of using dreams and symbolism as tools for self-knowledge, discovering how they can interpret these inner messages to support their path of liberation and rebirth.

Dreams are often deeply symbolic, drawing upon archetypes, personal memories, and emotions to weave narratives that reflect the dreamer's inner world. While some dreams may seem straightforward, others appear as abstract or surreal stories, and each has layers of meaning waiting to be uncovered. To begin working with dreams, participants are encouraged to keep a dream journal, placing a notebook beside their bed and recording any dreams immediately upon waking. Even a brief record—a few words or impressions—can capture essential details that may otherwise fade. Over time, as participants review their journal, recurring symbols or themes often emerge, revealing patterns or underlying emotional currents that may require attention.

In examining dream symbolism, participants can explore personal symbols—those unique to their own experiences and memories. For example, a person who associates water with childhood joy might interpret an ocean in their dreams as a symbol of emotional abundance or comfort. These personal symbols often hold memories or emotions specific to the dreamer, making them powerful guides for personal insight. To uncover the meaning of personal symbols, participants reflect on their own associations and memories, connecting these images to feelings or events in their lives. Through this process, they gain a personalized understanding of the language their subconscious uses to communicate.

Alongside personal symbols, universal symbols appear in dreams, tapping into collective archetypes that hold shared meanings across cultures. Symbols like mountains, representing obstacles or journeys, or snakes, symbolizing transformation or hidden knowledge, often appear in dreams as messages from the collective unconscious. By familiarizing themselves with these universal symbols, participants gain access to a broader spectrum of meaning, allowing them to interpret dreams as part of a universal narrative of growth and transformation. Working with both personal and universal symbols gives participants a fuller perspective, recognizing how their individual journey connects to greater, shared themes.

The presence of archetypes within dreams offers another layer of understanding, as archetypes represent core aspects of the human experience. Figures like the Hero, the Healer, or the Shadow often appear in dreams, each embodying qualities, fears, or desires the dreamer may need to explore or integrate. When an archetype emerges in a dream, participants can reflect on how this figure relates to their waking life, recognizing parts of themselves that may seek expression or healing. Engaging with these archetypal figures helps participants build a deeper connection with their inner world, allowing them to honor and work with the varied dimensions of their personality.

Participants may encounter recurring dreams, which often signal unresolved issues or persistent themes in need of attention. Recurring dreams frequently contain potent symbols, repeating until the dreamer confronts the underlying message. By examining these symbols and exploring how the recurring theme might relate to their current life, participants can often identify and address the root of unresolved emotions, releasing the dream pattern. Breaking free from recurring dreams often marks a release of tension or closure, reflecting a step forward in personal growth.

Once participants have recorded their dreams, interpretative techniques such as active imagination or dream dialogue offer a way to further engage with symbols or characters. In active imagination, participants revisit a dream scene while awake, entering a relaxed, meditative state where they can interact with symbols or figures from the dream. They might mentally ask a character questions, seeking deeper insight into the symbol's meaning or purpose. Dream dialogue takes this process further, where participants write out a conversation with a dream figure, allowing them to express curiosity, ask for guidance, and understand the message more fully. These techniques help participants bridge their waking and dreaming selves, creating an ongoing conversation with the subconscious.

Participants may also use visualization techniques to connect with the feelings or energies from their dreams. By visualizing specific dream scenes or symbols, they can bring the insights or sensations experienced in the dream into their conscious awareness. For instance, if a participant dreams of a peaceful forest, they might visualize this scene during meditation, embodying the sense of tranquility the forest provided. Visualization enables participants to access the emotional wisdom of their dreams, integrating its meaning into daily life and anchoring the dream's impact in their waking mind.

Additionally, setting intentions before sleep can guide participants toward receiving specific insights or clarity on questions. By focusing on a question or area of personal growth before bed—such as "What do I need to release?" or "How can I connect more deeply with my inner self?"—they create an invitation for their dreams to address these intentions. Though the response may not always appear immediately, consistent practice often yields dreams that provide answers, insights, or symbolic clues related to their intention. This practice establishes a relationship between the conscious and subconscious, building trust in the dream process as a source of guidance.

Interpreting dreams is a unique journey, and while participants can study symbolic meanings, the most profound insights often come from within. Personal intuition plays a vital role in dream interpretation, guiding participants toward meanings that resonate deeply with their own experience. Rather than relying solely on external interpretations, participants are encouraged to explore each dream symbol as it relates to their inner landscape, trusting their own associations and reflections. Dreams reveal meaning in layers, offering insights that may shift over time as the participant's self-awareness deepens.

In cultivating a regular practice of dreamwork, participants develop a greater understanding of their subconscious, bringing healing to aspects of themselves that may be hidden, suppressed, or unexplored. Dreams serve as messengers from within, providing glimpses into the complexities of the self and offering a path toward wholeness. As participants strengthen their relationship with their dreams, they learn to move fluidly between the worlds of conscious and subconscious, bringing clarity, growth, and healing to both realms.

By the end of this journey into dream symbolism, participants experience a profound connection with their inner lives, valuing dreams as meaningful expressions of their ongoing personal and spiritual journey. Dreams become allies on the path of transformation, guiding participants toward a greater understanding of themselves and deepening their sense of connection to the unseen depths of their psyche.

Building upon the foundational understanding of dreams and symbols, this chapter delves deeper into advanced techniques for interpreting, recording, and integrating dream insights into daily life. As participants continue to engage with their dreams, they learn to decipher complex layers of symbolism and gain access to their subconscious wisdom. This stage invites them to view their dreams as an ongoing, personal dialogue with their inner world, guiding their path of self-discovery and rebirth.

An effective approach for advanced dreamwork is the practice of lucid dreaming. In lucid dreams, the dreamer becomes aware that they are dreaming and may even gain control over the dream's direction. This awareness allows participants to explore their subconscious with intention, addressing fears, seeking answers, or connecting with symbols directly. To cultivate lucidity, participants can practice reality checks during waking hours, such as asking themselves, "Am I dreaming?" while observing their surroundings. This habit, carried over into their dream state, can trigger awareness within a dream, allowing them to consciously engage with its content. Lucid dreaming offers participants a powerful tool for self-exploration, where they can face hidden fears, ask questions of dream figures, or simply explore their subconscious landscape with heightened awareness.

Dream incubation is another technique that deepens the connection between waking intentions and dream insights. Before sleep, participants focus on a specific question or theme they wish their dream to explore, setting a clear intention such as "Show me my true potential" or "Reveal what I need to heal." Writing this question or affirmation in a dream journal reinforces the focus. By consistently setting intentions, participants encourage their subconscious to respond through symbolic imagery or direct experiences in the dream state. Over time, dream incubation helps establish a dialogue between the conscious mind and the subconscious, allowing participants to address questions and challenges in an intuitive, symbolic realm.

As participants receive insights through their dreams, symbol mapping becomes a powerful tool for interpreting complex or recurring symbols. This process involves creating a visual "map" of symbols that appear in dreams over time, noting any patterns, connections, or evolving meanings. Participants may draw the symbols, record associated emotions, and note changes in their appearance or context. For example, a recurring mountain symbol might initially appear as an insurmountable obstacle but later as a place of peace or wisdom. By tracking these symbols over weeks or months, participants can trace their own personal evolution, seeing how their relationship with certain aspects of themselves transforms as they grow.

Group dream analysis is an additional method that offers a new perspective on personal dreams by inviting others to provide their interpretations. In a trusted group setting, participants may share a dream without personal context, allowing the group to explore the symbolism with fresh eyes. Each member offers insights or reflections on the symbols, allowing the dreamer to consider interpretations they might not have reached alone. Group analysis helps participants recognize universal aspects within their dreams and enriches their understanding of personal symbols, often revealing layers of meaning that resonate deeply. The group's collective insight can also illuminate connections between individual and shared experiences, fostering a sense of unity and collective wisdom.

Active engagement with dream symbols in waking life is a technique that bridges dream insights into tangible action. Participants identify a significant symbol or message from a recent dream and incorporate it into their day. For instance, if a dream included a symbol of a key, participants might carry a key in their pocket as a reminder to stay open to new possibilities. Alternatively, if they dream of a garden, they might spend time in nature, nurturing a connection with growth and renewal. By bringing symbols into the physical world, participants honor the messages of their dreams, reinforcing the lessons or energies they convey and integrating them into their daily lives.

To deepen the emotional impact of dreams, rituals of release and integration are introduced. If a dream reveals an unresolved emotion, such as sadness or anger, participants can create a simple ritual to acknowledge and release this energy. For example, writing a letter to a figure from the dream or releasing a symbol into nature can serve as a cathartic process. Similarly, if a dream symbolizes a new beginning, participants might light a candle or engage in an act of creation, symbolizing their acceptance of this new phase. These rituals affirm the personal significance of each dream, providing closure for past themes and celebrating new understandings.

Dream-inspired creative expression allows participants to honor the richness of their dreams through art, writing, or movement. Drawing a recurring symbol, writing poetry about a vivid dream scene, or creating music inspired by dream emotions can bring the dream experience into conscious form. Artistic expression gives voice to the symbolic language of the subconscious, enabling participants to interact with their dreams in a way that bypasses the need for logical analysis. This creative process often brings further insights, as participants reflect on their artistic expression and how it relates to their current life or emotional state.

Participants are also introduced to symbolic reflection journaling, where they select a symbol from a dream and explore its potential meanings through free writing. They might begin with questions such as, "What does this symbol represent in my life?" or "How does this symbol make me feel?" This reflective process allows them to uncover personal associations, memories, or beliefs linked to the symbol, often leading to new understandings about their subconscious patterns or desires. By engaging with dream symbols through writing, participants bring a deeper level of clarity to their subconscious messages, discovering insights that guide their conscious actions and perspectives.

To bring a comprehensive approach to dreamwork, participants practice reviewing dream cycles, observing how their dreams shift over time. By revisiting their dream journal regularly, they gain a broader perspective on their emotional and spiritual journey, seeing how certain themes arise, evolve, and ultimately find resolution. For example, recurring dreams of feeling lost might give way to dreams of finding guidance or feeling empowered. This process of reflection reveals how the subconscious mind processes transformation, giving participants a sense of progress and completion in their journey. Recognizing these cycles helps participants understand that their dreams act as reflections of their ongoing personal growth.

Finally, honoring the dream as a guide reinforces the trust and respect participants have cultivated for their subconscious. Each dream, whether lighthearted or challenging, becomes a trusted messenger on their path. Participants learn to approach dreams with gratitude, acknowledging the wisdom, healing, and guidance they offer. By embracing dreams as allies, they build a profound relationship with their inner world, gaining insight that strengthens their sense of purpose and self-awareness.

As participants continue to interpret, record, and reflect upon their dreams, they learn to navigate the landscape of their inner self with confidence and curiosity. Each dream brings them closer to a fuller understanding of their unique journey, illuminating the depths of their emotions, beliefs, and aspirations. Dreamwork becomes an invaluable part of their healing and transformation, guiding them through the cycles of self-discovery and helping them uncover the wisdom and potential within. Through this ongoing dialogue with the subconscious, participants unlock deeper layers of self-awareness and empowerment, carrying forward insights that inspire growth, resilience, and wholeness.

Chapter 19
Therapeutic Process

The elements of nature serve as profound allies in the healing journey, each with a unique energy that offers solace, insight, and renewal. By reconnecting with these fundamental forces—earth, water, fire, and air—participants enter a rhythm that resonates with the natural cycles of transformation and rebirth. As they engage in practices that utilize these elements, they attune to the subtle language of nature and recognize their place within the greater web of life. This chapter explores the therapeutic benefits of integrating nature's elements into the liberation process, establishing a foundation for rituals and practices that promote deep healing.

One of the most grounding connections is with the element of earth, which provides stability, security, and support. This element embodies patience and persistence, holding space for growth and renewal. Practitioners can connect with the earth by spending time barefoot on soil or grass, feeling the stability and energy of the ground. By practicing grounding exercises, such as sitting or lying on the earth and visualizing their energy merging with the soil beneath them, participants can release mental and emotional burdens, feeling held and nurtured. Earth-based practices often evoke a sense of belonging, reconnecting participants to the simple, steady support of nature's foundation.

Moving to the element of water, participants experience the fluidity and adaptability inherent in their own emotional states. Water symbolizes cleansing, release, and the subconscious mind's depth. Natural bodies of water—rivers, lakes, oceans—serve as spaces where participants can let go of accumulated emotional residue. A common practice is to stand beside or immerse in water, visualizing their emotions flowing away with each ripple or current. In this space, water acts as a mirror, reflecting and purifying the self. Practitioners may dip their hands or feet into water as part of a ritual, feeling the cool touch as a balm that gently washes away inner obstacles, helping them to let go and trust in the natural flow of life.

The element of fire introduces transformation, warmth, and power, representing the strength to change and evolve. Fire rituals have long been used for letting go of attachments and releasing old patterns. By lighting a candle or a small fire, participants can observe the flames and reflect on their inner strength and resilience. Writing down fears or outdated beliefs on paper and offering them to the flame provides a symbolic release, with the fire consuming and transmuting what no longer serves them. This practice deepens participants' connection to their will and passion, igniting a spark of renewal that inspires them to embrace their rebirth with courage and intention.

Air, the final element, offers clarity, inspiration, and breath—the bridge between the mind and spirit. Air's qualities of lightness and movement are reflected in breathwork practices, where conscious breathing brings participants into a calm, centered state. Being outdoors, where the wind gently stirs or gusts with intensity, reminds them of the power of breath to move and release stagnant energy. Practitioners might practice deep, rhythmic breathing while facing the breeze, imagining the air filling their lungs with new insights and wisdom, and exhaling tension or mental clutter. This element provides a profound sense of mental clarity, as the breath opens pathways to insight and creativity, essential to the liberation process.

In addition to individual elemental practices, spending time in natural environments that combine these forces—such as a forest, beach, or mountainside—amplifies the therapeutic impact. The layered presence of earth, water, fire (in the sun), and air invites participants to explore the natural symphony of these energies, feeling a profound sense of harmony and interconnectedness. Simple activities, like walking mindfully on a forest path or sitting by the ocean, create space for reflection and grounding, reinforcing their connection to nature and self.

Beyond these sensory experiences, engaging with nature heightens awareness of seasonal cycles, reminding participants of their own capacity for growth and renewal. Observing the rhythms of blooming, decay, and regeneration in plants and trees teaches patience and acceptance, encouraging them to embrace their own cycles of change. Practitioners are invited to take time each season to connect with the changing landscape, noting how their own energy shifts in response. In spring, for example, they might focus on planting intentions, while autumn invites reflection and release. Following these natural cycles, participants align with the flow of life, understanding that transformation is both inevitable and beautiful.

As they deepen their relationship with nature, participants may discover personalized nature rituals that speak to their unique journey. These can include building small altars with natural objects—stones, leaves, or shells—as representations of intentions or aspirations. Creating these simple altars in natural spaces or at home connects them to the energy of the element or season they wish to honor, serving as touchstones for their personal growth. Additionally, planting seeds or tending to a garden offers a symbolic way to cultivate their inner transformation, witnessing the nurturing process as a reminder of their own growth.

Ultimately, nature-based practices bring a sense of wholeness, helping participants reclaim their place in the natural world. As they release the barriers that separate them from nature's wisdom, they become more attuned to their intuitive guidance and inner strength. Each element serves as a mirror, showing them aspects of themselves in the land, water, fire, and air. Through this recognition, they find resilience, clarity, and inspiration, rooted in the support of nature's rhythms.

As participants continue their journey, they deepen their commitment to their healing, learning to listen to the language of the natural world and honoring the balance it reflects. Nature's elements provide a constant reminder of the beauty and power of transformation, showing them how to move forward with harmony, trust, and an open heart. Through these practices, they step into alignment with the rhythms of life, embracing liberation and rebirth as both a personal and universal journey.

As participants deepen their practice of nature-based healing, they begin integrating specific, intentional rituals involving each of the elements—earth, water, fire, and air—to support the process of liberation and rebirth. These rituals foster a profound connection with the natural world, facilitating emotional release, self-reflection, and the embodiment of transformative energy. This chapter guides participants through advanced therapeutic practices with the elements, offering detailed rituals that harmonize their inner healing journey with nature's wisdom.

Connecting with earth through grounding practices nurtures stability and safety, anchoring participants as they release and transform. An advanced earth ritual, the Rooting Ceremony, begins with participants finding a quiet space outdoors, preferably near trees or stones, where they can sit or stand with bare feet on the ground. They are encouraged to visualize roots extending from the soles of their feet deep into the earth, feeling the grounding energy flow upward. This practice connects them to the earth's strength and stability, anchoring their intentions. As they breathe, participants envision any excess emotional energy, stress, or fear moving down their "roots" and being absorbed by the earth, transformed into grounding support. This ritual reinforces participants' sense of resilience, helping them find a foundation of trust and stability.

In the realm of water, practices that incorporate flowing movements or immersion in natural bodies of water create a symbolic and literal cleansing of the self. The Water Purification Ritual invites participants to release emotional burdens in a body of water, such as a river, lake, or even the ocean. Standing at the edge of the water, they hold in mind any emotions or beliefs they wish to let go of. As they step into the water, they imagine the cool liquid washing away all that no longer serves them. With each breath, they feel their emotional weight lessen, carried away by the current. For those unable to access natural water, a similar ritual can be done with a bowl of water, dipping hands and visualizing release. This cleansing ritual connects participants to their emotional fluidity, promoting clarity and renewal as they embrace the symbolic flow of water.

The fire element represents the energy of transformation and empowerment, a potent force for those ready to step into new identities. In the Candle Release Ritual, participants gather a candle, paper, and pen, writing down thoughts, fears, or patterns they are ready to release. After lighting the candle, they hold the paper near the flame, symbolizing the transfer of energy. As the flame consumes the paper, participants witness the transformation of their release, feeling a surge of renewed strength. Watching the paper burn, they focus on letting go with gratitude, acknowledging how each experience has contributed to their growth. Fire's transformative power ignites participants' will to move forward, allowing them to embrace change with courage and determination.

Air practices provide clarity and insight, as well as a sense of freedom from mental burdens. A powerful Breath of Clarity Ritual can be done outdoors, in a place where participants can feel the breeze. Standing with eyes closed, they begin with deep, rhythmic breaths, focusing on the sensation of air filling their lungs. Each inhalation invites clarity and openness; each exhalation releases thoughts, tension, or mental fog. To deepen the ritual, participants might incorporate visualizations, seeing each breath as a wave of energy clearing their mind. As they attune to the subtle power of air, participants experience a shift in perspective, fostering a clear and focused mental state that supports their journey forward.

For a comprehensive elemental experience, participants might engage in the Four Elements Ritual, aligning with earth, water, fire, and air in a single session. This ritual begins with grounding on the earth, connecting to stability, followed by cleansing with water, either by washing hands or using a small bowl. Next, they light a candle to symbolize inner strength and transformation, and finally, complete the ritual with a series of mindful breaths, honoring the air element. This holistic practice unites the qualities of each element, anchoring participants in a balanced state and supporting a full-body experience of liberation. By engaging all four elements, they gain a sense of wholeness, drawing strength from each natural force as they integrate their rebirth.

Another advanced practice, Creating a Nature Mandala, draws upon natural objects to represent the journey of rebirth. Participants gather stones, leaves, flowers, and other items found in nature, arranging them into a circular pattern that reflects their inner journey. As they place each object, they reflect on a specific aspect of their transformation—gratitude, healing, new intentions. This mandala becomes a symbolic mirror of their path, showing them how each phase of their journey forms part of a greater whole. Once complete, participants may sit beside their mandala in meditation, absorbing its energy before leaving it as an offering to nature.

As a way to close these nature rituals, the Gratitude Walk helps participants honor the land, elements, and themselves. Walking slowly through a natural space, they pay attention to the sights, sounds, and sensations around them, silently offering thanks. This walk reinforces the bond they have formed with nature, affirming their commitment to stay connected with the world around them. Each step becomes an acknowledgment of their healing and transformation, grounding them in a space of reverence for the journey they have undertaken.

These advanced nature-based practices guide participants into an ever-deepening relationship with their own healing and growth. Each ritual brings them closer to the elements, reinforcing their awareness that they are part of a vast, interconnected cycle of life, death, and rebirth. In connecting with earth, water, fire, and air, they find allies in their journey, reflecting back the power of resilience, fluidity, courage, and clarity.

As participants move forward, they carry the wisdom of the elements within, knowing that they can return to these practices whenever they seek grounding, cleansing, inspiration, or release. This relationship with nature becomes an ongoing source of strength and insight, reminding them of their own inner resources. With each ritual, they weave the energy of the natural world into their being, supporting their journey of liberation and rebirth with a foundation that is as timeless and enduring as nature itself.

Chapter 20
Artistic Expression

Artistic expression serves as a profound gateway to self-discovery, offering participants a way to release repressed emotions, explore subconscious insights, and integrate transformative experiences. Engaging in creative activities like drawing, writing, or music allows them to access parts of the psyche that words alone cannot reach, tapping into the layers of intuition, memory, and emotion. In this chapter, participants begin using creativity as a tool for self-healing, discovering how art becomes an intimate expression of their liberation journey.

Creativity arises from a place beyond the logical mind, a space where raw emotion, deep intuition, and unconscious memories reside. Participants often find that when they create without expectations or goals, they naturally bring forth aspects of their inner world. This process of "flow," or engaging in art without overthinking or censoring, invites spontaneous healing. By releasing any need for their art to "look" or "sound" a certain way, participants allow the creation itself to guide them. In these moments, art becomes a mirror, reflecting back symbols, themes, and feelings that reveal more than their conscious mind could articulate.

Drawing and painting are powerful ways for participants to access their emotions visually. When words feel insufficient, the use of color, shape, and form offers them a language to express what is within. A simple practice involves choosing colors that represent current feelings or moods and allowing the hand to move freely across the page, letting go of any need to create recognizable shapes. Through this method, the participants' inner landscape begins to reveal itself, with colors and strokes capturing the essence of their emotions—whether calm, vibrant, dark, or chaotic. After completing the artwork, they can spend a few moments reflecting on what has emerged, asking themselves questions about the colors, shapes, and patterns that appear, and noting any emotions or memories that arise.

Writing as artistic expression taps into the narrative mind, helping participants explore and reframe their experiences. One method, stream-of-consciousness writing, encourages them to write continuously without stopping, allowing thoughts, feelings, and images to pour onto the page without judgment. This practice often leads to surprising revelations, as emotions or insights previously held beneath the surface rise to the forefront. Another approach, dialogue writing, invites participants to engage in a "conversation" on paper with a part of themselves, perhaps an inner child, a symbol from a dream, or even an emotion like fear or joy. By "speaking" with these parts of themselves, participants gain insights, empathy, and new perspectives, uncovering layers of understanding that promote healing.

For some, music and sound become the channel through which emotions find release. Playing an instrument, humming, or even creating rhythmic beats allows them to express feelings beyond words. Participants may experiment with creating different rhythms to represent their current emotional state—soft, slow tones for introspection, or faster, more intense beats to release frustration or energy. For those without instruments, using the voice through hums, chants, or toning can be equally powerful. Sound holds a primal connection to emotion, vibrating through the body and resonating deeply within. Participants may find that simply allowing sound to flow freely shifts their mood, releasing tension or inspiring a sense of peace and balance.

Sculpture and tactile arts, such as working with clay, provide a grounding experience that connects participants to the physical body and the earth. The sensation of shaping, molding, and transforming a raw material mirrors the inner process of change and rebirth. Working with clay, for instance, allows them to externalize emotions, bringing form to feelings like sadness, anger, or hope. As they mold the clay, participants connect with the physical process of creation, witnessing their emotions take tangible shape. Once completed, they may choose to keep the sculpture as a symbolic reminder of their journey or let it go, symbolizing release and renewal.

Artistic expression often brings up unexpected symbols, figures, or shapes that carry personal meaning. To explore these symbols, participants can use symbolic reflection, where they take a particular image from their artwork—such as a recurring shape, color, or figure—and delve into what it represents to them personally. They may reflect on memories or associations related to the symbol, connecting it to past experiences or emotions. This approach allows participants to deepen their understanding of themselves, recognizing how these symbols reveal parts of their story, desires, or fears that seek expression and healing.

As they progress, participants may find it beneficial to set aside a specific time for creative rituals, treating their artistic practice as a sacred space. Creating a ritual around art—lighting a candle, using certain tools or colors—enhances the experience, inviting them to approach creativity with intention and mindfulness. In doing so, their art becomes more than expression; it becomes a ceremony of honoring their own growth and resilience. Participants can set intentions before beginning—such as releasing stress, gaining insight, or celebrating a personal strength—and let these intentions guide their art. With each brushstroke, word, or note, they reaffirm their commitment to healing and transformation.

Throughout this process, participants often experience a sense of self-compassion and forgiveness. When creating without judgment, they encounter parts of themselves that may have been suppressed or judged in the past. Art allows these aspects to come forward in a gentle way, fostering acceptance and understanding. Participants may create pieces that reflect painful memories or regrets, using art as a way to release and forgive. Over time, as they continue creating, they witness their own growth and resilience mirrored in their art, embracing a more compassionate view of themselves.

Artistic expression also serves as a record of transformation, allowing participants to look back on their work and see how their journey has evolved. Each drawing, poem, or melody marks a point along their path, capturing emotions and insights from specific moments in time. Reviewing past creations becomes a reflective practice, helping them see patterns, growth, and even resolution of past wounds. In this way, art not only facilitates healing in the present but also builds a personal archive that affirms their courage and progress.

Ultimately, art becomes a silent but powerful ally in the journey of liberation and rebirth. It offers a safe space where participants can explore, release, and transform their inner world, giving voice to parts of themselves that might otherwise remain hidden. Through artistic expression, they connect with their authentic self, celebrating both the struggles and the beauty of their personal path. This creative journey fosters self-awareness, empathy, and inner strength, creating a foundation upon which they continue to build their transformation.

As participants delve deeper into artistic expression, they move from spontaneous creation toward structured, intentional art therapy techniques designed to reveal, integrate, and transform complex emotional and spiritual experiences. These techniques encourage them to engage actively with the symbols, colors, words, and movements that emerge in their creative work, enabling a more profound dialogue with their inner world. In this chapter, participants learn advanced practices that use art as a transformative tool, facilitating self-awareness and healing as they bring hidden parts of themselves into the light.

One powerful technique in this stage of creative self-healing is visual narrative, a process where participants create a sequential story or series of images that depict their inner journey. This approach invites them to visualize and organize their feelings, memories, or insights as a series of moments or phases in their journey. Using a series of drawings, paintings, or collages, they depict different stages of their rebirth, such as moments of release, discovery, or newfound strength. As they add to this visual narrative over time, they begin to see patterns or cycles, recognizing phases of struggle and resolution. Each image represents a unique piece of their healing process, helping them to gain perspective on their progress and to acknowledge both challenges and victories.

Symbol mapping, or the conscious use of specific symbols within artwork, takes participants into deeper layers of self-knowledge. By choosing or creating symbols that represent particular emotions, relationships, or experiences, participants encode meaning into their art. For example, they might use a tree to symbolize growth, an open hand for acceptance, or a mountain for a significant challenge they face. With each art session, they map these symbols across various artworks, visually connecting the threads of their emotions and experiences. Over time, these symbols become part of a personal language that reveals patterns in their inner life, showing how certain emotions or memories are interconnected and, ultimately, helping them to gain a sense of mastery over complex feelings and themes.

Guided visualizations paired with art creation offer another way to deepen the therapeutic effects of artistic expression. Participants begin by engaging in a visualization exercise focused on an area they wish to explore, such as a memory, an unresolved emotion, or a source of inspiration. Guided visualizations lead them through imagery related to this area, allowing the subconscious mind to present symbols, colors, or scenes. After the visualization, participants transition directly into creating art based on the images and feelings that arose. This technique acts as a bridge between the subconscious and the conscious, allowing participants to access emotions and insights they might not reach through traditional reflection alone. The artwork that emerges often reveals a vivid, intuitive understanding of the self, enriched by the subconscious mind's input.

For those inclined toward writing, transformative storytelling is a method that allows participants to reframe and reinterpret personal experiences through the lens of narrative. By choosing a challenging experience, they create a story around it, imagining the journey from a perspective of healing and growth. They might envision a "hero" within themselves who faces and overcomes inner obstacles, or they might write about a past experience with a new understanding of its lessons. This storytelling process allows them to take a step back from their emotions, seeing their experiences as part of a larger journey. Through this reframing, participants find strength in their resilience and see meaning in moments of struggle, ultimately redefining their narrative with a sense of empowerment.

Another advanced practice is movement-based expression, where participants explore creative movement or dance as a means of embodying and releasing emotions. Movement bypasses the mind's filters, allowing participants to express emotions directly through the body. In a quiet space, they may begin by focusing on a feeling, such as frustration, peace, or joy, and then allow their body to move in ways that feel natural and expressive. No form or structure is necessary; the body leads, and participants follow its intuitive movements. This practice can be transformative, particularly for those who struggle to verbalize emotions, as it provides a safe way to express and release deep-seated energies. Movement becomes a way of embodying the process of liberation and rebirth, transforming abstract emotions into physical release.

The mask-making exercise invites participants to create a mask that represents an aspect of themselves they wish to explore, such as their inner child, their shadow, or their most empowered self. Using materials like clay, paper, or paint, participants design a mask that expresses this part of their psyche, including colors, textures, and symbols that reflect its unique qualities. Once complete, they can use the mask in role-play, embodying this aspect and exploring what it has to say. This exercise encourages participants to confront parts of themselves that may have been hidden or suppressed, allowing them to integrate these aspects into a balanced self-view. As they recognize and accept these parts of themselves, the mask serves as a visual reminder of their wholeness.

Collaborative art practices provide a way for participants to deepen their connection with others on a similar journey, whether in a workshop setting or with close friends and family. In collaborative art, each person contributes to a shared piece, such as a mural, collage, or sculpture, symbolizing mutual support and interconnected growth. This shared creative space allows participants to express vulnerability in a safe environment, experiencing the healing that arises from connection and mutual understanding. The completed artwork becomes a testament to collective strength, embodying the shared resilience and compassion that arise when individuals come together to support one another.

To honor and integrate the insights gained from these practices, participants can engage in a reflection and integration ritual with their artwork. After completing a piece, they spend time in silence, contemplating what it represents, what emotions arose during its creation, and what messages it holds. They may journal about the experience or engage in a meditation while observing the artwork, allowing the full impact of the process to settle within them. By revisiting the art in this way, participants create a bridge between the insight gained through creation and their everyday lives, ensuring that the lessons and healing continue to resonate.

As they engage in these advanced artistic practices, participants witness their own evolution reflected in their creations. Each piece of art becomes a step on their journey, a marker of self-discovery, healing, and transformation. In time, they build a rich archive of creative expressions that document their path of liberation and rebirth, bearing witness to their resilience and growth. This archive serves not only as a testament to their courage but also as a visual guide, reminding them of the depth of their journey and the power of their creativity to reveal and heal the self.

Ultimately, artistic expression transforms from a therapeutic practice into a lifelong tool for self-reflection and growth. With each brushstroke, movement, or word, participants continue to explore their own depths, understanding that healing is an ongoing, living process. Through art, they embrace a dynamic relationship with themselves, one that evolves and adapts as they do, offering a continual source of insight, liberation, and renewal.

Chapter 21
Personal Boundaries and Overcoming

In the journey of self-liberation, personal boundaries emerge as guardians of inner peace and self-respect. They represent the protective lines each individual establishes to uphold their emotional, physical, and spiritual well-being, delineating the space necessary for personal growth and freedom. However, boundaries are often influenced by past experiences, societal expectations, and personal fears, which may limit one's sense of autonomy or create a barrier to meaningful connections. In this chapter, participants explore the nature of their own boundaries, recognizing where these lines serve them and where they may be hindering their path to wholeness.

The process of identifying boundaries begins with self-awareness—acknowledging and honoring one's needs, values, and limits. This initial exploration reveals whether certain boundaries stem from authentic self-protection or from unresolved wounds or past conditioning. Participants are encouraged to reflect on moments in their lives where they felt uncomfortable, disrespected, or depleted. These instances often signal areas where boundaries may have been unclear or weak. Conversely, situations where they feel safe, respected, and energized suggest healthy boundaries that protect and nurture their well-being.

A key exercise in this self-reflection is boundary journaling, where participants document experiences and relationships that evoke feelings of discomfort or ease. By identifying these patterns, they begin to understand the areas in which they may need firmer boundaries or, alternatively, where they could allow themselves more freedom. Through this journaling practice, participants gain clarity on the underlying motivations and fears that shape their boundaries. They may notice, for instance, boundaries formed from fear of rejection, an instinct to overprotect, or a reluctance to trust. This awareness becomes the first step toward reshaping these boundaries to serve their present needs and growth.

Exploring boundaries inevitably involves facing self-imposed limitations—internalized beliefs and patterns that create a restrictive sense of self. Many individuals hold limiting beliefs about what they can achieve, how much joy they deserve, or how deeply they can connect with others. Often, these beliefs stem from past experiences or external judgments that were internalized over time. By examining these limitations closely, participants identify which beliefs no longer serve them and how these boundaries can be redefined. This self-inquiry leads to the realization that boundaries should be flexible rather than rigid, adaptable to the flow of personal evolution.

An essential practice in overcoming limiting beliefs is affirmation and visualization. Participants identify the limiting thought or belief they wish to release, then create a positive affirmation that represents its opposite. For instance, a participant who feels unworthy of love might affirm, "I am deserving of love and acceptance just as I am." During visualization exercises, they imagine themselves embodying this new belief, visualizing scenarios where they feel supported, respected, and confident. By practicing these affirmations and visualizations, participants reinforce their commitment to releasing limiting boundaries and embracing a sense of personal empowerment.

The concept of energetic boundaries is also introduced, emphasizing the importance of protecting one's energy while remaining open to meaningful interactions. Participants learn to tune into their own energetic field, sensing when interactions feel draining or nourishing. They are guided in creating a personal ritual that establishes a boundary of energy protection, such as visualizing a sphere of light surrounding them. This light serves as a buffer, filtering out negative or draining energies while allowing positive, supportive connections. By cultivating this practice, participants gain a tool that respects their need for personal space while promoting a balanced exchange of energy in relationships.

For many, setting boundaries with others—family, friends, colleagues—can be challenging. The boundary communication exercise encourages participants to assert their needs and boundaries respectfully and clearly. They practice expressing boundaries in a way that feels authentic and empowered, using "I" statements to communicate feelings without assigning blame. For example, instead of saying, "You never listen to me," they might say, "I feel unheard when I'm interrupted." This approach invites understanding and mutual respect, as the focus remains on the individual's needs rather than criticizing or controlling the other person's actions.

At the same time, participants are encouraged to explore the boundaries they have built within themselves—inner walls that might prevent them from accessing certain emotions, desires, or aspects of their personality. These inner boundaries may have developed as coping mechanisms, protecting them from vulnerability or perceived weakness. By slowly dismantling these walls, participants uncover parts of themselves that may have been long-hidden, allowing for a fuller experience of life. Through self-compassion practices, they learn to extend understanding to these aspects, integrating them into their self-concept with kindness and openness.

As participants become more attuned to their boundaries, they also develop a deeper appreciation for balance and adaptability. Rather than viewing boundaries as static, they recognize that personal limits may change according to life circumstances and inner growth. The boundaries that were essential in one phase of life may shift as they evolve, becoming more flexible or firm depending on new needs. This adaptability fosters resilience, helping participants stay attuned to their true self while remaining open to life's dynamic nature.

In honoring and refining their personal boundaries, participants begin to cultivate a sense of inner sovereignty—the realization that they hold the power to shape their lives, relationships, and self-concept. Boundaries become a way to protect this sovereignty without isolating themselves from meaningful connections. This newfound autonomy enables them to experience intimacy and trust in a balanced, empowering way, establishing connections rooted in mutual respect and integrity.

Ultimately, the exploration of boundaries leads participants toward a liberated sense of self, where they are neither constrained by excessive rigidity nor compromised by a lack of self-respect. As they redefine these boundaries with awareness and intention, they make space for authentic expression, deeper connection, and sustained personal growth. By overcoming limiting boundaries and embracing a fluid, empowered approach, participants step into a greater sense of freedom, building a foundation for ongoing transformation.

As participants continue the journey of redefining personal boundaries, they transition from awareness into practical application, learning advanced techniques for setting, communicating, and honoring boundaries in daily life. This deepened exploration invites them to release the self-imposed limitations they have identified, to transcend fears, and to cultivate a sense of empowered self-respect and openness. Through intentional practices, participants integrate boundaries not only as safeguards but as pathways to a balanced, fulfilling life.

One essential approach to sustaining healthy boundaries is through mindful embodiment practices. By tuning into the sensations and signals of the body, participants can identify when a boundary is being approached or crossed, often before they become fully conscious of it. In a simple practice of mindful scanning, they bring attention to areas of tension or discomfort that might signal emotional or energetic boundaries being compromised. For example, a tightness in the stomach may indicate discomfort with a situation, while tension in the chest may point to feelings of vulnerability. By noticing and honoring these signals, participants can intervene early, adjusting their responses in ways that support their well-being.

To support this attunement, grounding exercises provide a way for participants to reconnect with their center whenever they feel their boundaries are tested. Grounding involves focusing on the present moment through physical connection to the earth or mindful breathing, reminding the individual of their inner strength and stability. Participants might envision roots extending from their body into the earth, feeling anchored and immovable. This practice is especially helpful in challenging interactions or environments where boundaries might otherwise become blurred or difficult to uphold.

In the realm of relationships, assertive communication techniques empower participants to express boundaries without fear of conflict or rejection. They practice using direct yet compassionate language, focusing on personal needs rather than judgments of others. A foundational aspect of assertive communication is the use of "I" statements, which allow participants to express their experiences without attributing blame. For example, saying "I need some quiet time to recharge" instead of "You're always too loud" reframes the request in a way that encourages understanding and reduces defensiveness. Participants explore variations of these statements, gaining confidence in communicating needs calmly and directly.

Boundary rituals become another tool for reinforcing personal limits in situations where verbal communication may not be feasible or sufficient. These rituals can be as simple as setting an intention before entering a social situation or as detailed as creating a mental visualization to prepare for potentially challenging interactions. For instance, participants might envision a protective sphere of light surrounding them, offering a sense of security that allows them to engage without feeling overwhelmed. This visualization serves as a reminder that they can protect their energy while remaining open and present.

In overcoming boundaries rooted in fear or past trauma, exposure and gradual release exercises provide a way to challenge these limitations in a controlled, compassionate manner. Participants begin by identifying specific situations or interactions that feel intimidating due to past experiences. Then, they set incremental goals, gradually exposing themselves to these situations in manageable steps. For example, someone who struggles with public speaking might start by speaking in a small, trusted group, gradually building confidence before addressing larger audiences. With each step, participants affirm their ability to confront and transcend old limitations, replacing fear with resilience.

A particularly transformative exercise in this journey is the creation of personal mantras or affirmations, which serve as verbal reminders of their growth and strength. Participants choose statements that counter old fears and reinforce their commitment to boundary integrity, such as "I am worthy of respect," or "I honor my needs with confidence." Repeating these mantras during moments of doubt reinforces self-trust, helping participants internalize a sense of self-worth that naturally strengthens their boundaries.

As participants become skilled in setting boundaries with others, they turn inward, exploring the boundaries they hold with themselves—the often-unnoticed limits they place on their own potential, creativity, and self-expression. They confront questions such as, "What am I withholding from myself out of fear?" or "How do I limit my own freedom?" By recognizing these inner boundaries, participants identify self-imposed restrictions that no longer serve them. Techniques like mirror work, where they affirm self-worth while looking at their own reflection, help break down these internal barriers, inviting a fuller experience of self-acceptance and expression.

Forgiveness practices allow participants to release any guilt or regret surrounding past instances where boundaries were unclear or compromised. Holding onto guilt from past boundary violations, whether due to lack of awareness or external pressure, can create self-imposed boundaries based on shame. By practicing forgiveness, participants acknowledge their growth and release attachment to past mistakes. Through guided visualizations or journaling exercises, they cultivate a compassionate view of their journey, recognizing that every experience has contributed to their present strength and understanding.

For many, meditative boundary visualization becomes a practice to close the day, providing a moment to review and reinforce their commitment to boundary integrity. In this visualization, participants recall interactions and experiences from the day, noting instances where they upheld their boundaries and moments where adjustments might be beneficial. With each reflection, they visualize their boundary as a permeable yet resilient layer—one that allows positive, nurturing connections while filtering out negativity. This closing ritual encourages a gentle, self-reflective approach, helping participants feel grounded and empowered as they continue forward.

The practice of giving and receiving feedback further refines their boundary work, as participants learn to communicate their boundaries while remaining receptive to those of others. In group settings or one-on-one interactions, they practice articulating their needs clearly while remaining open to constructive feedback. This mutual exchange builds respect and understanding, reinforcing a healthy dynamic of both autonomy and connection. Learning to offer and accept feedback with grace strengthens boundaries by fostering trust and openness in relationships.

As participants integrate these techniques, they embody flexibility and resilience, realizing that boundaries are not static, unchanging walls but living aspects of their personal evolution. Rather than isolating themselves within rigid boundaries, they embrace an adaptable approach, tuning into their needs and adjusting their boundaries as life unfolds. This flexibility becomes a source of inner strength, reminding them that boundaries are meant to support their growth, not restrict their experience.

In mastering personal boundaries, participants unlock the power to live authentically, navigating life with both strength and openness. They embrace their right to protect their well-being while allowing meaningful connections to flourish. By releasing limiting boundaries and embracing a balanced, empowered approach, participants enter a new phase of freedom, ready to honor themselves and their journey with clarity and integrity.

Chapter 22
Building a New Identity

The journey toward building a new identity unfolds as a profound act of self-creation. Throughout liberation and rebirth therapy, participants have unraveled layers of self that were bound by old patterns, inherited beliefs, and past traumas. As these layers fall away, they enter a transformative space where the essence of who they are becomes clear and alive. This chapter invites participants to consciously construct an identity aligned with their authentic essence, guiding them toward a vision of self that resonates with their deepest values, aspirations, and personal truths.

In beginning this process, participants engage with a foundational exercise known as the essence discovery practice. Here, they are encouraged to reflect on the qualities and values they admire most—not only in others but also in themselves, often from memories or moments when they felt fully aligned with their inner self. They may recall times of kindness, courage, wisdom, or resilience and observe how these qualities felt, both physically and emotionally. By meditating on these core aspects, participants develop a clearer image of the values that form the bedrock of their new identity.

The act of visualization becomes central to shaping this renewed identity. Participants close their eyes and visualize their ideal self in great detail, imagining how they would interact, how they would respond to challenges, and how they would express their purpose. Guided by these reflections, they begin to imagine this self in real-life scenarios, seeing the characteristics that naturally emerge. In these visualizations, participants focus on embodying these traits, witnessing themselves as resilient, compassionate, or wise, affirming that these qualities are within reach and an intrinsic part of who they are.

Through identity affirmation exercises, participants create personalized affirmations that align with their vision. Statements such as "I am resilient," "I am guided by compassion," or "I am open to learning" help solidify the traits they seek to embody. Repeating these affirmations in the morning or before sleep serves as a daily ritual, imprinting these beliefs on the subconscious mind and supporting the gradual integration of these qualities into their sense of self.

A vital element in the creation of a new identity is letting go of limiting narratives—stories or labels that others may have placed on them or that they may have internalized over time. Through reflective journaling, participants write down beliefs they once held about themselves, such as "I'm not worthy of success" or "I need to be perfect to be loved." They confront these beliefs, questioning their validity and exploring where these narratives originated. This exploration reveals that many of these stories are not inherent to who they are but rather residues of past experiences. By acknowledging and releasing these narratives, participants free themselves to redefine their identity in alignment with who they wish to become.

Another technique that strengthens this new identity is role experimentation. Participants select specific scenarios in which they consciously embody their emerging traits. They might choose to approach a challenging conversation with assertiveness or express creativity in a new project. These intentional experiments serve as affirmations in action, reinforcing the qualities they wish to integrate into their everyday life. Each experience builds confidence and trust in their ability to embody this new self, proving that the change they seek is not a distant possibility but an unfolding reality.

Participants are encouraged to create a vision board or symbolic representation of their new identity. This board might include images, words, or items that resonate with their values, aspirations, and the qualities they aim to cultivate. Having a tangible reminder of their intentions reinforces their commitment and serves as a daily inspiration. This creative exercise helps participants ground their vision in something concrete, encouraging them to engage with their goals visually and emotionally.

Embracing vulnerability becomes another core practice in building a new identity. The path to self-creation often involves moments of uncertainty or discomfort, as participants move beyond familiar roles and step into new aspects of self-expression. Here, vulnerability is not seen as a weakness but as an honest exploration of self, allowing participants to grow with compassion and patience. In this way, vulnerability becomes a bridge to authentic connection, both with themselves and others, as they learn to navigate their identity with self-acceptance rather than rigid expectations.

In the later stages of this chapter, future self-dialogue offers participants a method to deepen their connection with this evolving identity. In a meditative state, they envision their future self—the one who has fully integrated these desired qualities. They allow this future self to offer guidance, support, or insights, asking questions such as, "How did you overcome self-doubt?" or "What brought you closer to your purpose?" By engaging in this internal dialogue, participants tap into the wisdom they already hold, bridging the gap between who they are now and who they aspire to become.

Through each exercise, participants are reminded that identity is a fluid, evolving creation rather than a fixed label. They learn that building a new identity does not mean abandoning past experiences or aspects of self but rather integrating all parts into a coherent whole that supports their growth. Each step in this process invites them to view their life as a canvas, with each choice and each interaction serving as brushstrokes that bring their vision into being.

In creating a new identity, participants realize they are not defined by the limitations or labels of the past. They discover a sense of empowerment that comes from aligning with a purpose and embracing values that resonate deeply within. With each insight, they step closer to a self that is not only liberated but also infused with purpose, fully prepared to navigate life with authenticity, courage, and an unwavering sense of self.

As one embarks on the journey of reinforcing life purpose, the newly formed identity begins to anchor itself in profound commitment. Here, the path transforms from mere intention to a reality deeply connected to the individual's mission, as they embody this purpose in every choice, relationship, and aspiration. In this chapter, the focus shifts from conceptualizing identity to the practical, grounded work of establishing a personal sense of purpose as the core of one's being.

The initial task in this integration is aligning with values. Building on reflections from prior practices, individuals assess how their evolving identity resonates with fundamental values such as integrity, compassion, and resilience. Through journaling exercises, they explore how these values have shaped key life moments, noting the inner alignment and harmony they felt when living authentically. Recognizing these values as the foundation of identity enables them to connect with actions that feel purposeful and aligned. Each value becomes a thread in the fabric of their identity, strengthening the commitment to a life that reflects this core essence.

In parallel, vision exercises become vital tools for reinforcing purpose. Through guided visualizations, individuals explore the future from the perspective of their highest self. They witness their interactions, contributions, and experiences as this renewed self, imagining how their choices reflect their identity. This exercise encourages them to see life not merely as a series of goals but as an unfolding journey, each step a testament to their true self. These visualizations serve as an intuitive roadmap, drawing forth both clarity and motivation to remain committed to the path.

Next, individuals engage in purpose-driven goal setting, transforming abstract intentions into concrete steps. Participants outline small, actionable goals in different areas of life—work, relationships, personal growth—that mirror their newly established purpose. Rather than setting conventional goals, they are encouraged to ask questions such as, "How will this action bring me closer to authenticity?" or "Does this goal reflect my core values?" This reflective approach to goal setting keeps them grounded in purpose, ensuring that each pursuit reinforces their evolving identity.

In sustaining this identity, daily rituals play a pivotal role. Mindful routines—whether morning affirmations, evening gratitude practices, or silent meditative moments—reinforce commitment by grounding the identity in daily life. These rituals serve as a gentle reminder, keeping one connected to the higher self even amid routine challenges. This ritual practice becomes sacred, a space where one's intentions and purpose are revisited, nurtured, and refined with each day's experiences. Over time, these rituals provide strength, resilience, and continuity, weaving purpose into the rhythm of life.

Additionally, reaffirmation practices solidify the newly constructed self. Through affirmations crafted around their purpose, individuals focus on phrases that empower their mission, such as, "I am guided by purpose and clarity" or "Every day, I grow closer to my truest self." These are repeated in reflective states, perhaps during meditation or as part of their morning routine. The affirmations help dissolve residual doubts and remind the mind and heart of the journey they've committed to.

As the new identity strengthens, the concept of service emerges naturally. Embracing one's purpose often inspires a desire to share this growth with others, be it through kindness, mentorship, or simple acts of compassion. Service becomes an extension of the purpose itself—a way to express identity in ways that bring meaning and connection. Each act of service reinforces the journey, offering fulfillment and helping individuals see themselves reflected in others' experiences.

Self-compassion remains a guiding force. In constructing an identity, the inner critic often surfaces, pointing out perceived inconsistencies or lapses. But here, self-compassion allows the journey to continue with grace. This isn't about reaching a state of perfection; it's about moving closer to one's true self with patience. By forgiving perceived setbacks and embracing growth as a natural, sometimes nonlinear process, individuals retain a balanced commitment to their purpose.

Finally, individuals reflect on their personal life mission statement, encapsulating their journey in a sentence or two that becomes a compass in times of uncertainty. This statement, evolving from prior exercises and values explorations, captures their essence and direction, serving as a beacon. Through it, they hold a sense of direction, an ever-present reminder that their actions and decisions align with their authentic self.

Thus, purpose becomes more than a goal; it becomes an unfolding, a continuous commitment to live in harmony with one's highest intentions. Here, life itself transforms—an evolving journey not only of self-discovery but of deeply intentional, purpose-driven living. With each new experience, each choice, the self is renewed, evolving in alignment with the deeper call to live authentically, fearlessly, and wholeheartedly.

Chapter 23
Practical Application

In the quiet stillness after transformation, a new journey begins—the journey of applying profound inner work to the rhythm of daily life. Integrating spiritual insights into routine moments brings both challenge and opportunity. With every interaction, task, and relationship, the opportunity emerges to infuse the day-to-day with intentionality, bridging the sacred space of ritual with the living pulse of daily existence. Here, the practice of liberation extends into practical realms, anchoring the growth achieved through each step of the therapeutic journey.

The first step in this application centers on mindful observation. Through consciously tuning into the present moment, individuals recognize habitual reactions, patterns, and energies in themselves and others. During routine activities—whether preparing a meal, commuting, or speaking with a friend—mindfulness invites a heightened awareness of thoughts, emotions, and responses. This practice isn't about changing one's nature but observing with curiosity and compassion. Each instance of mindful awareness deepens understanding and softens inner rigidity, providing a gentle reminder that the essence of transformation lies in one's choice of response, even in the most ordinary moments.

Through intention setting, practitioners bring clarity to each day. Here, small daily intentions become the focal points, guiding interactions and behaviors in ways that reflect their truest self. The intention might be as simple as "approach each task with patience" or "listen deeply to others." Setting these intentions each morning, perhaps accompanied by breathwork or quiet reflection, channels the energy from holistic practices into the rhythm of everyday life. This consistent practice of intentionality helps individuals remain anchored in purpose even when circumstances test their resolve.

Emotional grounding techniques serve as tools to navigate moments of stress or overwhelm. In a world that demands so much of one's energy, practices such as deep breathing, grounding visualizations, or even brief moments of stillness reconnect individuals to their core. By returning to the breath in difficult moments or mentally visualizing roots anchoring them to the earth, practitioners regain balance and release unnecessary tension. This grounding brings a sense of safety and calm, ensuring they can approach each moment from a place of centered strength, allowing for clear thinking and calm decision-making even amid external pressures.

The practice of energetic boundaries becomes crucial in protecting one's newfound self-awareness. In navigating relationships and environments, individuals may encounter others' emotions or energies that can disrupt their internal peace. Here, visualization techniques—such as imagining a protective light or energetic shield—help maintain the individual's emotional clarity without absorbing external negativity. This boundary is not one of isolation but of mindful protection, allowing practitioners to engage meaningfully with others while preserving the sanctity of their inner journey.

Equally important is authentic communication. As one's understanding of self deepens, so too does the capacity for honest, heartfelt communication. Practitioners begin to approach conversations with openness and empathy, listening without judgment and expressing themselves with authenticity. In moments of discord or misunderstanding, this form of communication fosters clarity and fosters trust. Authentic communication emerges as a natural extension of inner peace, creating a ripple of harmony that extends through personal and professional interactions alike.

To reinforce these practices, reflection periods offer opportunities to observe, adapt, and appreciate progress. In these moments of solitude—whether through journaling, meditation, or quiet contemplation—individuals revisit the day's events, examining choices and responses. Here, the day's small victories, missed opportunities, and challenges become stepping stones for future growth. This practice fosters gratitude for progress, reinforcing that the application of inner work is a journey of continual refinement, one in which each day offers a new opportunity for integration.

As these practices take root, practitioners explore purposeful connection with others. Acts of kindness, understanding, or simple presence remind them of their place within the interconnected web of humanity. In these connections, they find that living authentically inspires others, creating a gentle ripple effect. Even simple gestures, such as offering encouragement or holding space for someone's experience, become a reflection of the liberation they've nurtured within themselves. This commitment to connection reminds individuals that their growth is not a solitary endeavor but a contribution to the collective.

In weaving these practices together, balance and resilience arise naturally. The practitioner learns to flow through challenges without losing sight of their core, maintaining equilibrium through life's peaks and valleys. Resilience is not about rigidly holding to an ideal but adapting gracefully, integrating the lessons of each experience. They come to trust in their journey, knowing that each day offers growth and renewal, embodying the transformation as a quiet, steady presence.

Through these practical applications, the self finds expression in all dimensions of life, allowing inner growth to blossom outward. By bridging the profound work of liberation with everyday choices and interactions, the practitioner embodies a harmonious alignment with self and world. The spiritual and the mundane converge, creating a life that is not only lived but deeply, intentionally experienced.

As the journey deepens, the practices for sustaining growth and transformation find their way into daily rhythms. Here, we expand on the tools that maintain the essence of liberation in ordinary life, nurturing a continuum of self-awareness and intentional living. This ongoing cultivation anchors the spirit of rebirth, reinforcing the sacred connection between self and world, moment by moment.

To begin, daily rituals of presence serve as consistent reminders of one's inner path. Small, deliberate acts—lighting a candle in the morning, pausing with gratitude at mealtimes, or spending a few moments in stillness—root the practitioner in a mindful state. Such rituals transcend their simplicity; they act as anchors, aligning intentions with actions and inviting presence into each unfolding day. These practices weave the insights of liberation into the fabric of daily experience, creating a rhythm that keeps practitioners attuned to their core, no matter the external pace.

The art of reflective journaling provides a structured space to capture and examine the subtle shifts that emerge through practice. Each entry becomes an opportunity to acknowledge growth, identify recurring patterns, and explore emotional landscapes. Reflection opens a dialogue between the conscious mind and the depths of the heart, cultivating self-awareness and granting insight into the flow of internal and external dynamics. Journaling can further serve as a repository for dreams, intuitive insights, or fleeting inspirations, grounding these ephemeral glimpses in a tangible form that can be revisited and drawn upon in times of need.

In parallel, goal-setting and intentional planning transform lofty aspirations into actionable steps. By articulating both short-term and long-term intentions, practitioners harness the creative power of focused energy, directing it toward purposeful ends. This process is not merely about setting milestones; it becomes a dialogue between vision and action. Goals rooted in personal values create a guiding framework, shaping the contours of daily life to reflect the soul's intentions. Such planning fosters accountability, grounding the expansive potential of inner work in the practical actions that define a life lived with purpose.

Central to sustaining growth is breathwork and mindful movement. Practices like yoga, tai chi, or mindful walking cultivate an integrated state where body and mind function as one. Moving with intentional awareness strengthens the body, frees the mind, and deepens the practitioner's connection to self. Breath becomes both a compass and an anchor, directing energy, grounding emotions, and dissolving tension. These physical practices nurture resilience, granting practitioners a reliable means of recentering when life's demands create strain.

Equally vital is the maintenance of energetic hygiene. Through techniques of visualization and intentional cleansing—like visualizing a protective light or releasing stagnant energy through breath—practitioners keep their personal energy field clear and balanced. Tools such as crystals, smudging with sage, or sound healing add depth to this practice, cultivating a space of clarity and openness. This energetic upkeep not only protects against external influences but also strengthens the internal equilibrium essential for enduring transformation.

Interpersonal dynamics take on new meaning as practitioners integrate these practices. Mindful listening and compassionate engagement emerge naturally as extensions of the inner journey, reshaping relationships into authentic exchanges. By honoring others' experiences without judgment and expressing one's truth with integrity, the practitioner fosters an environment of mutual respect and understanding. Such relationships, rooted in shared presence, become fertile ground for healing, growth, and genuine connection.

As practitioners progress, ongoing self-compassion practices fortify their journey. Recognizing moments of self-doubt, forgiving perceived missteps, and holding space for vulnerability become acts of nurturing the self. Self-compassion becomes a bedrock that supports resilience, granting the grace to meet each moment with kindness. In this way, liberation extends inward as well as outward, strengthening an enduring sense of worth and peace within.

In the spirit of liberation, periodic personal reviews foster continuity, inviting practitioners to assess the effectiveness of their practices and realign where needed. These check-ins create space for evaluating growth and celebrating the victories, no matter how small. Reviews are opportunities to renew commitments, recalibrate goals, and refine practices to support the path ahead. They offer a gentle pause, grounding the journey in clarity and reaffirming the practitioner's dedication to conscious evolution.

Lastly, connection to community serves as both inspiration and support. Engaging with like-minded individuals offers camaraderie, encouragement, and shared wisdom, enriching one's journey through the diversity of shared experiences. Community connections offer both an external mirror and an inner wellspring, deepening the understanding that the work of liberation contributes not only to personal growth but to the collective journey toward healing and wholeness. Practitioners find in community a reminder that their journey is part of something far greater, a rhythm shared by all who seek authenticity and healing.

Through these layered practices, practitioners nurture a dynamic cycle of awareness, growth, and renewal. Each tool is both a grounding force and a bridge, supporting the continuity of inner transformation while inviting it into the tangible reality of everyday life. In this way, the journey becomes a lived expression of liberation, extending the sacred from ritual spaces into the heart of the daily experience.

Chapter 24
Integration of Transformation

As the journey through liberation and rebirth deepens, a subtle transformation emerges, one that reaches beyond ritual and practice, settling into the rhythms of daily existence. This phase of integration is not about grasping for a new way of life but rather allowing a gentle, natural unfolding that brings the insights, clarity, and awakenings experienced into each moment. The process is delicate and gradual, requiring a surrender to a new flow, a reorientation of the self that resonates with authenticity and newfound strength.

At the heart of this integration lies the concept of conscious embodiment, where the truths discovered within are no longer confined to moments of meditation or ritual but infuse the everyday—actions, thoughts, interactions—with a sense of sacred intentionality. Practitioners may find themselves naturally gravitating toward choices and behaviors that reflect their inner journey: a tendency toward kindness, a patience rooted in compassion, or a stillness that pervades even the busiest of days. These changes are subtle yet profound, weaving the sacred into the most ordinary experiences.

An essential part of this transformation involves awareness of one's own energy, learning to notice and honor fluctuations in mental and emotional states without resistance. In moments of challenge or stress, practitioners find that the practices of breathing, grounding, and presence become vital tools that reconnect them with their center. In these moments, the body and mind are no longer separate from the journey but active participants, each sensation, each emotion pointing toward deeper layers of healing and self-discovery.

Another integral aspect is intentional reflection—a daily or weekly practice of pausing to acknowledge growth, to celebrate the subtle shifts and new understandings that emerge. Reflection fosters appreciation for the journey itself, recognizing that each step, no matter how small, contributes to a larger transformation. Through journaling, quiet contemplation, or simply revisiting significant moments, practitioners develop a mindful relationship with their progress, one that acknowledges the journey's ebb and flow without judgment.

Connection with nature becomes a grounding force, as practitioners draw from the natural world's cycles to anchor their own process of renewal. The simplicity of spending time outdoors, of feeling the earth beneath one's feet, of witnessing the changing seasons, reinforces the organic rhythm of transformation. Nature serves as both a mirror and a guide, a reminder that growth unfolds in its own time and that, like all things, the path of integration is a delicate dance of persistence and patience.

The concept of service to others also gains new dimensions, as practitioners discover that sharing their journey, even in small ways, nurtures their own growth while uplifting those around them. Whether through active listening, small acts of kindness, or simply embodying the peace they've cultivated, each interaction becomes an opportunity to extend the principles of liberation outward. In this way, the process of integration reaches beyond the self, resonating within the lives touched by each practitioner's transformed presence.

Balancing inner and outer lives emerges as both a challenge and a gift. Practitioners begin to navigate the equilibrium between personal rituals of growth and the demands of daily responsibilities. This balance invites flexibility, a gentle give-and-take that respects both the commitment to inner development and the reality of outer obligations. In maintaining this harmony, the journey transforms from a separate endeavor into a seamless thread woven throughout each area of life, making the practice of liberation an integral, lived experience.

The art of releasing control comes naturally as practitioners embrace the understanding that true transformation is not a destination but a state of being. Trust in the journey itself becomes the guiding principle, allowing life's mysteries and uncertainties to unfold without resistance. This surrender brings with it a freedom, an openness to the unexpected, a willingness to grow without precondition.

In moments of solitude, self-compassion becomes a nurturing balm. The journey into transformation is not without its challenges, and self-compassion allows practitioners to embrace moments of struggle as necessary parts of their growth. Through forgiveness, kindness, and patience with oneself, the practitioner's path becomes one of gentle acceptance, where each step is honored, and each misstep is met with understanding.

Through these practices and more, integration weaves the insights of liberation into the heart of everyday life. The inner world finds resonance in the outer world, not as two separate spheres but as a unified whole. In this phase, transformation is no longer something that happens in moments of ritual or meditation but a state of being that permeates every thought, every interaction, every breath. In the quiet embrace of this awareness, the journey of liberation continues, unfolding in harmony with life's rhythm, complete in its simplicity, profound in its subtlety.

As transformation continues to blend into the fabric of daily life, a nuanced layer of intentionality takes root. This phase is marked by a conscious practice of anchoring transformative insights, so they become second nature—a quiet power that weaves itself into every action, word, and thought. Practitioners are encouraged to cultivate a life where each moment, however mundane, becomes a portal to this inner alignment, creating a seamless flow between their inner and outer worlds.

One way to deepen this integration is through mindful embodiment exercises. These practices are simple yet potent, involving an intentional focus on the sensations and energies that arise within the body in everyday situations. Through movements like walking or stretching, practitioners bring their awareness to the experience of being fully present, grounded in their bodies. In each step or breath, a renewed sense of clarity and inner balance emerges, grounding the transformative shifts in the physical form. Such embodiment becomes a gentle reminder that every insight, every awakening, exists not only in the mind but also as a resonance within the body.

A complementary practice is morning intention-setting, a brief ritual at the start of each day. Practitioners silently connect to their deeper intentions, aligning with their goals of growth, self-awareness, and harmony. This practice does not necessarily require formal meditation but can be a simple pause, a moment of stillness where they reconnect with the essence of their transformation. By setting a clear, heartfelt intention, practitioners carry an anchor throughout the day, a reminder of their path that subtly guides each choice and reaction, infusing the day with purpose.

Another powerful tool in this phase is evening reflection, where practitioners quietly review their day with compassion and curiosity. They recall moments when they felt aligned with their transformative path and moments when they might have strayed. Rather than judging or critiquing, they observe, acknowledging these instances as reflections of their current state. By noting the subtleties of their experiences, practitioners gain insight into their evolving nature, learning to celebrate growth while embracing any setbacks with kindness. This practice fosters patience and self-compassion, reinforcing the belief that the journey is not linear but an unfolding spiral of progress and self-discovery.

Energy renewal practices also play a crucial role in sustaining transformation. Throughout the day, practitioners can engage in brief resets—whether through mindful breathing, a quiet moment in nature, or a few moments of meditation. These small yet potent rituals act as checkpoints, realigning the inner self with the transformative process, restoring balance, and releasing any accumulated tension. Over time, these practices become instinctive, offering a wellspring of inner peace that is ever-present and immediately accessible.

As these practices take root, the presence of expanded self-awareness naturally becomes apparent. Practitioners develop a refined sensitivity to their emotional and mental states, recognizing patterns and responses that may have once gone unnoticed. In this space of heightened awareness, they can identify and release lingering attachments or unhelpful thought patterns. They learn to witness emotions with detachment, understanding that feelings are passing experiences rather than fixed aspects of self. This liberating awareness deepens inner peace, helping practitioners navigate life's challenges with grace and perspective.

To integrate transformation fully, mindful communication emerges as an invaluable tool. Practitioners approach each interaction as an extension of their inner journey, practicing active listening, openness, and compassion. They become conscious of their words and tone, choosing language that reflects their transformation and encourages harmony. Through these mindful exchanges, they can maintain their connection to their authentic selves, even in challenging conversations, grounding themselves in the compassion and wisdom they've cultivated.

In addition to these daily practices, symbols and reminders of transformation can serve as touchstones in the physical world, reinforcing inner alignment. These could be as simple as a chosen object or a piece of art that reflects their journey. Such items act as gentle prompts, bringing them back to their intentions throughout the day, especially in moments of distraction or challenge. A symbol placed in a significant space can reconnect them with their path, drawing their focus back to the profound work they have undertaken.

Embracing stillness in all its forms completes the practice of integration. Through quiet reflection, solitude, or a few moments of undisturbed silence, practitioners find space to truly listen to the subtleties within. This stillness becomes a sacred pause, a reminder that beneath the ebbs and flows of transformation lies a place of unchanging peace—a sanctuary that can be accessed at any time.

In this chapter of integration, transformation ceases to be a distant ideal or abstract concept. Instead, it becomes the silent force behind each thought, word, and action, a light that gently guides life's unfolding. Practitioners embrace this quiet power, knowing that transformation is both the journey and the destination, held within each present moment. And with this realization, their journey into liberation and rebirth reaches a state of peaceful fulfillment, as life itself becomes a practice of living one's deepest truth.

Chapter 25
Reinforcing Identity and Confidence

As the journey of transformation unfolds, a profound shift in identity begins to take shape, one rooted in authenticity and resilience. This new identity is not merely a set of beliefs or self-descriptions but a tangible, living force that guides actions and responses. It embodies the essence of the liberation journey—a release from old confines and an embrace of self as an ever-evolving being.

Building confidence in this emerging self requires both self-awareness and self-trust. To anchor this confidence, practitioners first reconnect with moments when they have experienced personal strength and integrity. Through journaling or quiet reflection, they recall times when they acted from a place of courage or compassion. These moments become foundational stones in the structure of their new identity, memories that remind them of their capacity to stand firm and act authentically.

This reflection is complemented by visualization exercises that expand self-awareness. Practitioners begin by visualizing their renewed self in daily life, embodying qualities they value and aspire to cultivate—whether empathy, assertiveness, patience, or clarity. These visualizations are not fantasies; rather, they are practiced experiences that familiarize the mind and body with this new way of being. Each time the visualization is repeated, the essence of the self is strengthened, resonating on a deeper level.

In tandem with visualization, affirmation practices reinforce this identity, especially when paired with breath or body awareness. These affirmations are crafted carefully, not merely to boost mood but to resonate with the core values that have emerged through transformation. Instead of general affirmations, practitioners choose words that resonate with their personal truths—statements that acknowledge both their journey and the essence of their renewed self. By grounding these affirmations in breath or touch, they bridge the gap between thought and feeling, creating a powerful reminder of their identity.

As confidence builds, a practice of mindful boundaries becomes essential to maintaining this inner alignment. Practitioners learn to protect their energy, discerning when to engage with external influences and when to maintain distance. Through observing their interactions and recognizing any signs of energy drain or misalignment, they develop a refined sense of personal space. This practice is not about withdrawal but rather about sustaining the integrity of the self by honoring its needs and limitations.

Throughout this process, practitioners may also experience the subtle yet potent effects of mirror work. This practice invites them to face themselves with acceptance and compassion, examining their own eyes in a mirror and observing what arises. It is a practice that reveals any lingering hesitations or self-doubt, allowing these to surface so they can be gently released. In facing their own reflection, practitioners reinforce the self-acceptance and compassion that are central to this chapter's teachings.

These practices encourage an alignment with self-empowerment, a gentle yet unyielding force that becomes the core of their confidence. Practitioners learn to view their past, not as a shadow but as a foundation, supporting the person they have chosen to become.

As the practitioner's renewed identity takes shape, cultivating a resilient confidence becomes essential. This confidence is not solely outward strength; it is an enduring self-assurance grounded in self-awareness and deep inner conviction. To reinforce this, the practitioner engages in practices that nurture an alignment between intention and action, guiding the new self to express itself authentically.

In this part of the journey, one crucial exercise is affirmative visualization. Here, the practitioner imagines their life as it unfolds through the lens of this renewed identity. As they visualize the essence of this self navigating both anticipated challenges and unknown paths, they sense its qualities—its calm presence, thoughtful responses, and unwavering resilience. With each visualization, these qualities root deeper, guiding the practitioner toward intuitive and mindful reactions, especially in difficult or complex moments.

This identity is also strengthened through a technique known as embodied affirmations. Rather than reciting affirmations passively, the practitioner integrates them through physicality—standing tall, moving deliberately, and breathing deeply as they affirm their sense of purpose. By connecting thoughts to action, these affirmations resonate throughout the body, supporting the practitioner's confidence and grounding it in their physical experience. Each affirmation then becomes a lived expression, reflecting the inner transformation in tangible ways.

Another powerful tool in this phase is the practice of reframing. This involves shifting perspectives on past limitations or perceived failures, viewing them as steps in a greater journey. With reframing, the practitioner observes previous moments not as obstacles but as opportunities for growth, signs of resilience that led to this profound evolution. Through journaling or reflection, they rewrite these experiences, releasing self-doubt and honoring the courage it took to reach this new self. In recognizing this strength, the practitioner solidifies their commitment to an empowered identity.

In moments of quiet, the practitioner may also turn to inner dialogue as a practice of self-acknowledgment. Through intentional dialogue with the self, they express gratitude, support, and understanding, fostering self-compassion and reinforcing their sense of worth. This practice serves as a reminder that the inner voice is a source of encouragement, cultivating an intimate space where the practitioner feels safe, valued, and capable of facing new challenges with confidence.

Throughout this journey, mindful action becomes a daily ritual that extends beyond personal practice, encouraging the practitioner to integrate their new identity into relationships, work, and life. Each interaction, no matter how small, is a reflection of this self-empowered individual. Whether it is through mindful listening, acting with patience, or setting gentle but firm boundaries, the practitioner's renewed identity becomes visible, creating harmony between their inner self and the external world.

In moments of stillness, the practitioner finds connection with the greater tapestry of life. Through meditative practices, they dissolve the boundaries of individual identity, sensing themselves as part of something vast and interconnected. This understanding fosters humility and assurance, recognizing that their journey is both unique and universal. With each breath, they feel at ease with their renewed self, grounded and resilient, ready to continue growing with confidence and inner strength.

Chapter 26
Self-Compassion Practices

In the realm of profound personal healing, self-compassion is a gentle yet powerful force. It invites the practitioner to view themselves with kindness and acceptance, as they would a beloved friend. This inner kindness doesn't simply offer comfort; it becomes the foundation for a deep and lasting healing, transforming the way one perceives and interacts with their own vulnerabilities.

The journey into self-compassion begins with mindful acknowledgment of the self. The practitioner learns to observe emotions and thoughts without judgment, releasing the urge to categorize them as "good" or "bad." This practice asks for openness, a willingness to see one's imperfections without resistance or critique. Here, the practitioner discovers that emotions, even those seen as unpleasant, are part of the spectrum of human experience. By honoring all parts of the self, they find that acceptance naturally begins to emerge.

An essential practice within this chapter is the self-compassion meditation. As the practitioner settles into a calm, quiet space, they are guided to place a gentle hand over their heart and tune into their breath. This gesture of physical connection reinforces a sense of warmth and tenderness. As they breathe, they might softly repeat words of compassion, such as "May I be kind to myself" or "May I accept myself as I am." With each breath, these words resonate within, allowing compassion to permeate the heart. Gradually, this meditation becomes a refuge where they can return whenever self-judgment arises.

The practitioner also learns the art of self-forgiveness, which opens the door to releasing self-blame or past regrets. In this practice, they may visualize a younger version of themselves—someone in need of understanding and kindness. By bringing this image to mind, they acknowledge the struggles, fears, and mistakes of their younger self with a sense of patience. This exercise enables them to recognize that each choice and experience has contributed to their growth, encouraging a release of guilt and the gentle embrace of acceptance.

Self-compassion also extends into the body through somatic self-care. The practitioner is encouraged to notice where they carry tension or emotional heaviness. With focused breath and gentle movement, they bring awareness to these areas, releasing held energies that may have long gone unnoticed. This mindful physical care nurtures the body with the same compassion afforded to the mind and heart, honoring the interconnected nature of healing.

Another potent technique is writing letters of compassion to oneself. The practitioner takes time to write a letter addressing their own pain or self-criticism as they would to a friend. In this letter, they acknowledge struggles, express encouragement, and offer understanding. This practice provides a tangible reflection of self-compassion that can be read and reread, serving as a reminder of their inner ally. Through writing, the practitioner's compassion becomes something real, lasting, and deeply personal.

As the practitioner deepens into self-compassion, they begin to release the constraints of perfection. They come to see that flaws and struggles are not shortcomings but gateways to growth and understanding. This perspective, developed over time, allows them to embrace themselves more fully, transforming self-compassion from a practice into a way of being. And, in this acceptance, the path toward true healing unfolds.

The practice of self-compassion deepens into a more subtle yet profound journey, touching layers of the self that hold unspoken pains, dormant fears, and unresolved emotions. Here, the practitioner is encouraged to explore forgiveness—not as a simple release but as an act of liberation. Forgiveness, in this sense, becomes a way to dismantle self-imposed barriers, an acknowledgment of the humanity that resides within every aspect of oneself.

To facilitate this exploration, the practitioner engages in a reflective exercise: the mirror of self-forgiveness. This begins with the act of sitting before a mirror, meeting one's own gaze, and allowing feelings to surface without suppression. As they look into their own eyes, they are encouraged to speak words of forgiveness aloud: "I forgive you for the burdens you've carried," or "I forgive you for the moments you felt unworthy." By vocalizing these sentiments, the practitioner frees these burdens from within, creating an energetic shift that begins with simple acknowledgment.

In the flow of these exercises, a gentle yet transformative practice follows: metta or loving-kindness meditation, specifically directed toward the self. This ancient practice, rooted in compassion, invites the practitioner to silently repeat phrases that foster well-being, such as "May I be at peace," "May I be free from suffering," and "May I dwell in love." As these phrases are repeated, a warmth begins to grow within, filling spaces that once held judgment or doubt. The loving-kindness meditation, practiced regularly, fosters an ever-growing empathy within, a continuous offering of patience and kindness.

Alongside this meditation, another practice unfolds—releasing judgments through breathwork. Here, the practitioner focuses on the act of breathing, visualizing each exhale as a release of self-criticism or self-imposed limitations. With each exhale, they let go of thoughts like "I am not enough" or "I should have done more." The physicality of breath becomes a symbol of cleansing, gently dissolving rigid standards imposed on the self. In these moments, breath becomes the vehicle for compassion, nourishing and renewing the practitioner with each cycle.

Forgiveness through imagery is yet another avenue for self-compassion. In a relaxed state, the practitioner visualizes an encounter with a version of themselves burdened by regret or past mistakes. They envision approaching this version of themselves with love, embracing it, and allowing any painful memories to dissipate like mist. By offering this compassionate embrace, they acknowledge that all past actions, thoughts, and feelings contributed to their growth. This visualization gently releases the residual energies that cling to these memories, making space for healing.

To solidify these practices, compassion journaling is introduced. This reflective exercise guides the practitioner to record moments when self-judgment arises and to counteract each judgment with an expression of kindness or understanding. For instance, if they write, "I failed at this task," they respond with, "I did my best, and my worth is not defined by this moment." Over time, this journaling practice rewires the mind to seek compassion instinctively, creating a nurturing internal dialogue that supports resilience and grace.

As self-compassion practices deepen, the practitioner finds that these acts of kindness begin to permeate other aspects of their life. Relationships are experienced with greater empathy, and inner peace arises, replacing former unrest. Through these gentle, continuous acts of self-compassion, the practitioner not only heals but also fortifies the foundation upon which they stand, creating a new relationship with themselves that radiates acceptance and enduring kindness.

Chapter 27
Cultivating Gratitude

Gratitude, though often seen as a mere practice of politeness or fleeting moments of appreciation, unfolds here as a sacred and transformative state of consciousness. Within the liberation and rebirth journey, gratitude becomes a potent catalyst, one that nurtures resilience, shifts perspectives, and aligns the soul with the essence of life.

The journey into gratitude begins with simple moments of reflection, inviting the practitioner to cultivate awareness of the gifts already present in their life. The first step is learning to observe without expectation. As they enter into a calm state, the practitioner begins to notice the small and ordinary—the rhythm of their breath, the light filtering through a window, the comforting warmth of their body. Each element, though often overlooked, is honored, its presence acknowledged as part of the fabric of existence. This awareness opens a new layer of perception, guiding the practitioner to see their surroundings as interconnected, each element contributing to their present moment.

Another integral practice is intentional gratitude journaling. Here, the practitioner is encouraged to journal each morning or evening, recording moments of gratitude that emerged throughout the day. Yet, this isn't a mere list-making exercise; it is a ritual in which each written word carries intention. In expressing gratitude for a meal, a conversation, or even a challenge overcome, the practitioner deepens their connection with each experience, transforming fleeting moments into nourishing reflections. Over time, this journaling becomes a sacred dialogue, a reminder that each experience, whether joyful or challenging, carries purpose and meaning.

To further embed gratitude, the practice of mindful acknowledgment is introduced. During daily routines, the practitioner is guided to pause and mentally acknowledge the sources of each experience. If they are eating, they pause to acknowledge the earth's contribution to the food; if they are working, they reflect on the journey and skills that brought them to that moment. This simple act of acknowledgment shifts habitual thoughts, reminding the practitioner that each moment is sustained by a web of elements, seen and unseen.

In complement to this, the offering of gratitude through breath becomes a core practice. The practitioner closes their eyes, taking a slow, deliberate inhale, and on the exhale, they offer gratitude for something specific—a person, an experience, a quality within themselves. This cycle continues, with each breath extending gratitude, creating a rhythm that harmonizes the practitioner's inner state. Breath, already a source of life, becomes a vessel for appreciation, allowing the body to resonate with gratitude's energy. This practice, as it grows, becomes a refuge, a way to cultivate peace, even amid daily challenges.

One of the most profound gratitude practices introduced here is the ritual of compassionate reflection. In a calm, reflective state, the practitioner brings to mind past experiences, even those filled with hardship or regret, and explores how they contributed to their journey. With each memory, they identify a lesson learned, a strength cultivated, or a piece of wisdom gained. This ritual reframes past wounds not as burdens but as elements that, in some way, contributed to the person they are becoming. This approach transforms pain into wisdom, revealing that each part of their journey, regardless of its nature, offers something to be grateful for.

To deepen their practice, the practitioner is invited into acts of gratitude. This involves not only inward practices but also outward gestures, a way to share the gratitude cultivated within. Whether it is through a kind word, a small act of generosity, or a moment of listening, the practitioner brings gratitude to life, weaving it into their relationships and daily interactions. Each act reinforces that gratitude is not only an internal state but a gift that can be shared, creating ripples of connection and appreciation that extend beyond the self.

As these practices take root, gratitude reveals itself as a bridge—a means by which the practitioner not only appreciates what exists around them but also acknowledges their place within it. The world, once viewed through the lens of separation, begins to dissolve into unity, with each element, experience, and individual part of a greater whole. Through gratitude, the practitioner realizes that liberation is not solely about release, but also about the sacred act of receiving life with an open heart.

As gratitude deepens within, it transforms from a simple practice into a sustaining, powerful force, harmonizing each moment with a sense of purpose and interconnectedness. In this chapter, the practitioner learns advanced techniques to embed gratitude into their daily rhythms, allowing it to shape their worldview, interactions, and responses to life's complexities.

The path begins with guided visualization, a method for accessing gratitude's boundless potential by focusing on experiences and relationships that nourish and support. As the practitioner closes their eyes and centers themselves, they are guided to envision their life as a tapestry, where every person, lesson, and experience is a unique thread. This vision invites them to embrace their history with compassion and acknowledgment. In weaving each thread with gratitude, they begin to perceive their journey not as a series of isolated events but as a richly interconnected narrative, one that has molded their present self.

Building upon visualization, the practitioner is encouraged to explore gratitude through self-inquiry, asking profound questions that stir introspection and self-awareness. Questions like "What gifts have emerged from my greatest challenges?" and "What parts of myself am I grateful for today?" prompt the practitioner to see value in all aspects of their experience, even those previously overshadowed by doubt or pain. This exploration fosters resilience and compassion, unveiling strength within vulnerability and nurturing an enduring appreciation for their personal growth.

Another practice, gratitude through affirmations, anchors these realizations. Each day, the practitioner is guided to articulate specific affirmations that affirm their appreciation for life's abundance, both within and around them. By speaking these affirmations aloud or silently, they imprint gratitude into their conscious mind, which over time influences their subconscious. As these affirmations become routine, they infuse each day with an openness to receive and cherish, fortifying the practitioner's connection to gratitude even amid routine or difficulty.

Breath and energy alignment also play a vital role, as the practitioner integrates gratitude into their physical and energetic being. Through a series of intentional breaths, they are guided to imagine gratitude entering with each inhale, expanding through their body, and radiating outward with every exhale. This breathwork aligns not only the mind but also the body and spirit with gratitude's energy, clearing stagnation and enhancing the sense of lightness and peace within. This integration amplifies their capacity to respond with calmness and openness, transforming each interaction into a chance to express the gratitude that lives within.

Rituals of symbolic release are introduced for moments of past resentment or unresolved pain. Here, the practitioner visualizes these burdens as stones they have carried, consciously offering each one into an imagined river or flame as they whisper words of release and gratitude. This ritual not only allows the practitioner to acknowledge and let go of past wounds but also transforms each experience into a symbol of gratitude for the resilience it nurtured within them. Such releases lighten their energetic load, enabling a freer, more expansive connection to gratitude.

Gratitude's influence extends into the practice of intentional presence, a state where the practitioner actively focuses on the beauty and significance of each moment, no matter how mundane. By fully engaging their senses—feeling the warmth of sunlight, listening to a gentle breeze, or savoring a simple meal—they allow gratitude to emerge naturally. This active presence cultivates a profound awareness of life's subtleties, reminding them that each experience, when observed with intention, has something to offer.

To deepen their interaction with others, the ritual of shared gratitude is encouraged. Whether with friends, family, or even strangers, the practitioner learns to openly express thanks for the presence and contributions of those around them. This practice creates a shared space of appreciation, dissolving barriers and fostering genuine connection. By sharing gratitude, they not only enrich their relationships but also amplify gratitude's energy, allowing it to ripple outward and inspire others.

In the final practice of this journey, evening reflection becomes a sacred moment where the practitioner revisits the day with a heart open to gratitude. They are encouraged to recall specific moments, however small, that brought joy, comfort, or learning, expressing thanks for each one before sleep. This practice acts as a bridge between conscious awareness and the subconscious, guiding the mind into rest filled with a sense of contentment. Over time, this nightly gratitude reflection weaves itself into the fabric of the practitioner's being, creating a life rooted in appreciation and peace.

Through these deepened practices, gratitude transcends being an occasional feeling and becomes a guiding principle, a source of inner stability, and a light that illuminates every corner of the practitioner's life. As this state of thankfulness takes root, it nurtures a life lived with open-heartedness, resilience, and joy, aligning the practitioner ever more closely with their path of liberation and rebirth.

Chapter 28
Intentions for the Future

Standing at the threshold of a new phase, one feels the gentle yet profound stirrings of potential. This chapter leads practitioners through the foundational act of setting intentions for the future, harnessing self-awareness gained throughout the journey. In doing so, they establish a framework that aligns their actions, emotions, and aspirations with their deeper self—a spiritual compass to navigate the unknown.

Intentions differ from goals in subtle but powerful ways. Unlike goals, which are often specific and measurable, intentions embody a broader vision of purpose, a commitment to live in alignment with one's values. Here, the practitioner is guided to clarify personal values, those intrinsic beliefs that fuel meaningful growth and connection. Through mindful reflection, they begin to understand that intentions are not just tasks to accomplish; they are principles to embody, ways of being that nurture self and spirit.

The journey of intention-setting begins with conscious self-reflection, an exploration that invites the practitioner to contemplate their life path, what they cherish most, and the direction in which they wish to grow. Questions emerge: What lights the spirit within? Which aspects of life bring harmony and peace? Through such inquiry, they cultivate an awareness that aligns their intentions with genuine desires, revealing a path that reflects their truest essence.

One powerful tool in this process is the ritual of envisioning. In this exercise, the practitioner visualizes their future as an open landscape—filled with colors, textures, and emotions that reflect the ideal path they wish to walk. They are encouraged to imagine themselves thriving, to see how they engage with the world around them, and to explore what they create and share with others. This vision serves not as a rigid destination but as an inspiration, one that fosters both resilience and flexibility. With each detail, they breathe life into their intentions, creating a mental and spiritual blueprint for the coming years.

Writing intentions becomes another sacred practice in which practitioners capture the essence of their vision. As they put pen to paper, the abstract takes form, and the future is infused with clarity and purpose. Writing solidifies intentions and creates a tangible reminder of the practitioner's commitment to their growth. Here, intentions are expressed in statements that are positive, affirmative, and present-tense, as though already realized: "I live in balance and harmony," "I embrace growth with courage," "I nurture connections that uplift and inspire." Through these words, they anchor their aspirations, empowering the spirit to act in alignment with the path envisioned.

To reinforce this alignment, the practitioner is encouraged to connect each intention with an elemental symbol, a token from nature that embodies the energy they wish to cultivate. A smooth river stone, for example, may symbolize resilience, grounding them in times of turbulence. A feather might represent freedom, encouraging lightness and flow. By placing these symbols in their daily environment, they invite gentle, constant reminders of their intentions. Each time they see or touch the object, they reconnect with the energy of their aspirations, making their intentions an active presence in the rhythm of life.

Intentions also hold deeper significance when shared within supportive communities, whether with friends, family, or trusted spiritual companions. In speaking intentions aloud, the practitioner strengthens their commitment and allows others to witness this moment of growth. This shared experience transforms intention-setting into a collective ritual, magnifying its impact through shared energy and accountability. As each person holds space for the other's aspirations, an environment of encouragement and collective strength blossoms.

Lastly, the chapter introduces the practice of periodic reflection, in which the practitioner is invited to revisit and reaffirm their intentions regularly. Life evolves, and so may one's vision and values. By setting aside time to reflect on the journey, to celebrate progress, and to recalibrate where needed, the practitioner ensures that their path remains dynamic, open to growth and adaptation. This commitment to ongoing reflection reinforces their intentions and renews their connection with the spirit of their purpose.

Through these practices, the act of setting intentions becomes a transformative ritual, one that embraces both the present moment and the promise of the future. In moving forward with clarity, practitioners create a harmonious link between their present self and the path ahead, guided by the light of their deepest aspirations.

As the journey of setting intentions deepens, the practitioner finds themselves drawn into a process of grounding and action, where the visions of the future weave into the fabric of daily life. Intentions, which began as whispers of desire, now call for conscious steps toward realization, demanding both commitment and the active engagement of the spirit. This chapter delves into practical tools and mindful practices that allow practitioners to embody their intentions and craft a life in alignment with their inner truths.

One begins by creating an action map, a unique guide that traces the path between the present moment and the envisioned future. This is not a conventional roadmap; rather, it is a visual expression of where the spirit feels drawn. The practitioner is encouraged to draw, write, or symbolically outline their vision, filling the map with markers that represent the milestones they hope to reach and the practices that will nurture their growth. As each marker reflects a personal commitment to transformation, this map becomes a sacred document, a constant reminder of the intentional path forward.

This is followed by the practice of setting small, achievable goals that align with the broader vision, infusing everyday life with moments of intentional progress. For each goal, the practitioner consciously considers its purpose and connection to their values, transforming each step into an offering of dedication to their intention. Each small achievement builds momentum, fostering confidence and reinforcing the faith in one's ability to manifest the envisioned life. Through these mindful steps, the once-distant vision begins to feel closer, more tangible, a part of everyday existence.

Daily rituals of affirmation are introduced as a way to maintain alignment with intentions throughout this journey. With focused presence, the practitioner recites affirmations that mirror their intentions, grounding each day in the energy of their desired path. These affirmations serve not only as words but as a steadying force, like a mantra that clears the mind and spirit, allowing the practitioner to remain resilient against the pull of distraction or doubt. Each spoken affirmation rekindles the commitment to the journey, fortifying the inner resolve to live in harmony with one's highest aspirations.

In harmony with affirmations, the practice of mindful visualization becomes a powerful tool to immerse oneself in the energy of the future self. This involves more than simply picturing a desired outcome; it is an active experience of embodying the emotions, thoughts, and behaviors that align with the practitioner's intentions. Visualization invites the practitioner to feel the joy, the peace, and the fulfillment of their envisioned path, transforming these qualities from distant possibilities into present realities. By regularly inhabiting the feelings associated with their intentions, they condition both body and spirit to move naturally toward these outcomes.

Central to this process is the cultivation of emotional resilience, as intentions often illuminate internal resistances or fears that arise along the journey. Here, the practitioner is encouraged to view each challenge as a mirror, reflecting aspects of self that may benefit from healing or acceptance. Through compassionate introspection, they address these resistances directly, transforming fear or doubt into learning experiences. Resilience becomes an ally, an unwavering companion that emboldens the practitioner to continue despite obstacles, deepening their sense of purpose and inner strength with every trial encountered.

As intentions grow into sustained practices, the chapter introduces periodic reflections, moments of pause in which the practitioner revisits their action map and assesses the journey thus far. These reflections allow for recalibration, honoring shifts in vision or desire, and embracing flexibility in the journey's unfolding. Here, the practitioner learns that change is not a divergence from the path but an integral part of it, an evolution of the soul's yearning that may refine or expand the original intentions. Through periodic reflection, they maintain a dialogue with their inner self, ensuring that each step remains authentic and meaningful.

An important ritual in this phase is the ceremony of commitment, a sacred space in which practitioners reaffirm their intentions. This ceremony is an invitation to honor the path chosen, speaking aloud their intentions in a moment of solitude or within a trusted circle, allowing the words to resonate as a vow to oneself. Whether under the open sky, near water, or within the warmth of candlelight, this ritual of declaration strengthens resolve, embedding intentions into the heart and mind with a powerful sense of dedication and respect.

Lastly, the practitioner is encouraged to integrate acts of gratitude into the journey, recognizing that the practice of setting and following intentions is a gift to self and to life. By cultivating gratitude for each moment of growth and learning, the practitioner imbues their journey with humility and joy, creating an energy of positivity that propels them forward. Gratitude deepens awareness of the progress made and fosters a sense of peace with the unfolding process, allowing the practitioner to appreciate each step, regardless of the pace or nature of the journey.

Through these tools and practices, intentions are no longer distant dreams but living truths, woven into the tapestry of each day. The practitioner moves forward not only with vision but with action, resilience, and a deep-rooted commitment to their path, trusting that each step taken in alignment with intention brings them closer to the harmonious and purposeful life they seek.

Chapter 29
Continuous Growth Cycle

Embarking on the continuous growth cycle, the practitioner senses an invitation to explore beyond the familiar landscape of transformation and enter a rhythm that is cyclical and boundless. Growth, in this form, is not linear but a spiral that ascends and deepens simultaneously, weaving together insights from past experiences and the potential of what is yet to be. With this understanding, the practitioner moves forward with a newfound awareness, learning to sustain and nurture growth as an ongoing process rather than a single destination.

In the heart of this continuous journey lies the practice of attuned self-observation, a gentle and compassionate attentiveness to one's inner world. Through this, the practitioner cultivates the ability to recognize subtle shifts in energy, emotions, and thoughts, observing without judgment. This self-awareness becomes a guiding light, illuminating the path of growth, as well as the areas of life that may need deeper exploration or healing. Self-observation is both mirror and map, revealing the textures of the spirit and offering direction as one moves through each stage of growth.

An essential part of this cycle is setting new intentions as old goals evolve or reach fulfillment. As the practitioner moves forward, they may find that the intentions once held have transformed, calling for fresh visions and aspirations that reflect their evolving sense of self. By consciously updating these intentions, they remain engaged with the continuous process of growth, recognizing that each cycle of rebirth brings with it a renewed understanding of purpose. Intentions, like seasons, are meant to shift, adapting to the deeper truths that emerge with time.

The practitioner is then encouraged to explore creative visualization as a means to actively engage with each stage of growth. Through visualization, they call upon the power of imagination to connect with possible futures, exploring how various paths and choices resonate within. In these inner journeys, they not only visualize outcomes but engage with the sensations, emotions, and transformations associated with them. This visualization process serves as a rehearsal, allowing the spirit to experience growth before it materializes in the physical realm, strengthening the bond between vision and reality.

As growth continues, there arises a natural rhythm of expansion and rest, which becomes a cornerstone of sustainable development. The practitioner learns to recognize periods of intense growth and transformation, balanced by intervals of rest and integration. This ebb and flow mirror the cycles found in nature, where growth requires time for reflection and renewal. The practitioner is encouraged to honor these phases, trusting that each rest period allows for insights and wisdom to crystallize, nurturing the foundation for the next wave of growth.

To support this continuous journey, rituals of grounding become vital practices. Whether through meditation, connection with nature, or mindful movement, grounding helps the practitioner to remain centered and connected to the present, especially as growth may bring moments of uncertainty or vulnerability. Grounding rituals provide stability, allowing the practitioner to feel rooted in their path even amidst transformative changes. These rituals serve as anchors, reaffirming the individual's connection to both the earth and the expansive potential of the spirit.

The cycle of growth is further enriched by periodic assessments, where the practitioner takes time to reflect on lessons learned, goals achieved, and areas for improvement. This reflective practice is not one of critique but of gentle acknowledgment, a recognition of the effort, resilience, and wisdom that have emerged. Through honest assessment, the practitioner identifies patterns and discovers ways to approach future cycles of growth with even greater awareness and balance, fine-tuning their approach to honor both self and spirit.

A unique aspect of this chapter focuses on practices of adaptability, which encourage the practitioner to approach growth with flexibility and openness. Growth, by nature, does not follow a rigid path; it is fluid and ever-changing, and the ability to adapt becomes essential. Here, the practitioner learns to let go of expectations, allowing growth to unfold in its own time and manner. Adaptability becomes a gift, transforming obstacles into opportunities, and each unexpected twist becomes a chance to discover deeper strengths and insights.

Supporting this adaptability is the introduction of journaling as a companion practice. By documenting thoughts, emotions, and realizations, the practitioner builds a personal archive of growth, capturing the nuances of each cycle. Journaling creates a sacred space for reflection, where one can revisit past entries, recognizing patterns and changes that may have gone unnoticed. It becomes a dialogue with the self, a means of tracking transformation and celebrating the often-subtle ways growth manifests.

In embracing this continuous growth cycle, the practitioner also begins to develop a relationship with impermanence. Recognizing that all phases, achievements, and challenges are transient allows for a sense of peace and acceptance. Growth, in this sense, becomes a dance with the flow of life, free from attachment to specific outcomes. Embracing impermanence encourages the practitioner to move through each stage with gratitude, honoring the lessons learned and remaining open to the new journeys that await.

Through these practices, the continuous growth cycle becomes a living, breathing process, one that is renewed with each breath, each insight, and each intention. The practitioner learns that growth is not an endpoint but a sacred rhythm, a journey without end, wherein every step becomes both a departure and a return. In this cycle, they find freedom, knowing that growth is an eternal dance, a journey woven from the threads of discovery, resilience, and boundless potential.

As the practitioner immerses in the depths of the continuous growth cycle, the journey expands into a dimension of enduring practices and evolving awareness. This stage is one of deepening commitment, where daily life itself becomes a canvas for self-discovery and renewal. Each moment, however ordinary, reveals itself as an opportunity for growth—an ever-flowing invitation to explore, understand, and integrate.

At the core of this sustained growth lies the practice of daily presence. The practitioner cultivates a heightened awareness that extends beyond formal rituals or designated spaces, weaving mindfulness into the threads of everyday activities. Through this presence, the practitioner learns to view each experience—whether it be a simple conversation, a moment of solitude, or even a challenge—as an encounter with the self. This commitment to presence sharpens the practitioner's sensitivity to subtleties, enabling them to witness the gentle shifts and flows of their own growth.

Building upon this, mindful breathing serves as both anchor and guide. Breathing, practiced consciously, becomes a direct link to the present, a rhythm that mirrors life's cycles of ebb and flow. With each inhale, the practitioner welcomes renewal; with each exhale, they release stagnation. Breathing exercises are integrated throughout the day, providing grounding and clarity. This conscious breathing acts as a silent companion, guiding the practitioner back to their inner center, even amidst external noise and motion.

An essential component of sustained growth is the concept of adaptive resilience, where the practitioner embraces a flexible response to life's unfolding. As growth progresses, challenges arise, yet each difficulty reveals itself as a hidden teacher, offering lessons that deepen inner strength. Resilience is not about resisting change but about bending with it—meeting life's transitions with a spirit that adapts and evolves. Through resilience, the practitioner learns to find equilibrium, a grounded center that remains steady even as external circumstances shift and transform.

In this part of the growth cycle, energy renewal practices take on a heightened significance. Growth, especially when sustained, requires careful management of one's energetic resources to avoid fatigue or imbalance. The practitioner explores techniques such as grounding meditations, light physical movement, and immersion in nature to refresh and sustain vitality. Each renewal practice acts as a fountain, replenishing the practitioner's reserves, ensuring that growth unfolds with ease rather than strain.

Community connection also emerges as a powerful catalyst for growth in this cycle. While much of the journey is deeply personal, sharing insights and experiences with others can bring fresh perspectives and encouragement. Practitioners are encouraged to find or create communities that resonate with their path, where mutual support and collective wisdom foster a shared environment for continuous evolution. In community, individual insights blend and amplify, creating a tapestry of shared experience that enriches each participant's journey.

Complementing community is the practice of self-compassion. In the continuous growth cycle, the practitioner learns to be as gentle with themselves as they would with others, embracing their own imperfections and honoring the stages of development they have yet to reach. Self-compassion allows them to navigate moments of self-doubt or fatigue, recognizing that growth is neither rapid nor uniform. This kindness toward the self acts as a balm, a nurturing force that encourages resilience and patience as the practitioner progresses.

Rituals of closure and renewal become valuable tools in this advanced stage. As growth is continuous, so too is the need to release aspects of the self that have served their purpose. These rituals involve intentional reflection on past experiences, releasing what is no longer needed, and setting intentions for the future. This process creates space within, a spiritual and emotional clearing that welcomes the next wave of transformation. Rituals of closure become acts of renewal, grounding the practitioner in a cycle that is forever evolving.

Exploration of creative practices deepens, providing a means for the practitioner to express and process their experiences. Through art, movement, or written reflection, creative practices allow the individual to translate the abstract aspects of growth into tangible form. Creativity becomes a language through which the practitioner communicates with their inner self, expressing emotions and insights that may be difficult to articulate otherwise. This practice also serves as a reminder that growth itself is a creative act, a continuous creation of one's identity and inner landscape.

Additionally, periodic retreats and reflections offer a structured pause in the cycle. These retreats, whether in solitude or with a community, are opportunities for immersion, allowing the practitioner to engage deeply with their inner journey. During these times, the practitioner steps away from the rhythm of daily life, entering a space where insights can be crystallized, intentions can be recalibrated, and connections to self and spirit can be reaffirmed. These retreats become sanctuaries, guiding the practitioner back to their core essence.

As growth becomes an inseparable aspect of life, the practitioner encounters the concept of spiritual humility. This humility is an acknowledgment of the vastness of growth, an understanding that no matter how far one has come, there is always more to discover. Spiritual humility opens the practitioner's heart to the unknown, to the mysteries of life and self that remain uncharted. It is this humility that keeps the practitioner grounded and open, allowing them to approach each stage with a beginner's mind, free from the illusion of completion.

In this sustained growth, there is also a gentle surrender to life's natural rhythms. The practitioner learns to recognize when to act and when to rest, honoring the cycles of nature as reflections of their own internal cycles. This connection to rhythm brings ease, a sense of flow that guides growth naturally, free from force or struggle. By aligning with life's rhythms, the practitioner finds balance, knowing that each season, each phase, is integral to the cycle of continuous growth.

In embracing these practices, the practitioner weaves an intricate relationship with their own evolution—a journey that transcends linear time, where growth is not a final destination but an infinite unfolding. Through continuous growth, they find a boundless path, a sacred cycle that echoes through each moment, whispering the promise of renewal and the eternal rhythm of self-discovery.

Chapter 30
Others on the Path to Rebirth

When one emerges from the depths of personal transformation, they may feel a profound calling to extend a hand to others. Guiding another soul on this path requires more than just knowledge or technique; it is a journey of humility, presence, and open-hearted listening. In this chapter, we explore the art of supporting others as they move through the phases of liberation and rebirth. This guidance is not the imparting of one's own truths, but rather the creation of a safe and sacred space in which each individual may discover their unique inner path.

At the heart of supporting others lies active listening, an art that goes beyond words. To listen actively is to attune oneself not just to the spoken narrative, but to the emotional and energetic undertones of each moment. This listening requires a stillness within the guide, a quieting of their own thoughts and biases, so that the practitioner's experience can unfold naturally. It is as if the guide becomes a mirror, one that reflects without distorting. Through this reflective presence, the individual on the journey feels seen, heard, and, most importantly, understood.

Empathy is the silent language of this connection. An empathetic presence allows the guide to feel with, rather than for, the other. In empathy, there is no space for judgment or preconceived solutions; there is only an openness to the complexity of human experience. The guide enters the terrain of the other's inner landscape with a sense of wonder and respect, acknowledging that each person's journey is as unique as their essence. Through empathy, a space of genuine connection arises—one where healing can root deeply, nourished by acceptance and trust.

Integral to the role of guiding others is the practice of holding space. To hold space is to create an environment where the practitioner feels safe to explore their inner world without fear of criticism or interference. This space is one of neutrality, where the guide's presence is neither directive nor passive but a calm anchor. Within this safe harbor, emotions can surface, stories can be told, and silence can be honored. The guide, in holding this space, cultivates a sanctuary in which vulnerability is not only allowed but welcomed.

Non-attachment emerges as a crucial principle in the support process. The guide learns to release the desire to influence outcomes or control the journey of the other. Instead, they trust in the wisdom of the practitioner's inner process. This non-attachment allows the practitioner to feel free, not confined by the expectations or desires of their guide. In this release, the guide witnesses the journey from a place of respect and openness, honoring each moment as it arises without clinging to specific results or transformations.

There is also the element of compassionate encouragement. While it is important to respect each person's pace, the guide may offer gentle encouragement, urging the practitioner to trust in their own resilience. This encouragement is not a push but a reminder of the strength within. When doubt arises, the guide's compassionate words can reignite the practitioner's confidence, reminding them of the courage that brought them to this path. Compassionate encouragement allows the guide to be a steady source of warmth, one that reassures without overwhelming.

A profound aspect of guiding others is the cultivation of boundaries. In order to support without absorbing the practitioner's emotional burdens, the guide must develop a clear sense of their own energetic boundaries. These boundaries protect both the guide and the practitioner, ensuring that the guide remains centered and balanced. Through this clarity, the guide models healthy boundaries, demonstrating that deep compassion and clear limits can coexist harmoniously. This balance sustains the guide's well-being, allowing them to continue offering presence without depletion.

The guide's role often includes facilitating self-reflection. Rather than offering direct answers or solutions, the guide gently redirects the practitioner's focus inward, encouraging them to seek answers within. This facilitation of introspection empowers the practitioner, reinforcing the belief that they are the ultimate authority in their own healing process. Through open-ended questions and thoughtful pauses, the guide leads the practitioner to their own insights, fostering a deepening trust in their inner wisdom.

A key part of supporting others in rebirth is celebrating small victories. The path of liberation is not marked solely by grand revelations or dramatic shifts; it is also built on quiet moments of clarity and small steps forward. By acknowledging these small victories, the guide nurtures a spirit of encouragement and acknowledgment. Each step, however modest, is an affirmation of the practitioner's commitment to growth, and the guide's recognition reinforces the practitioner's confidence in their progress.

The guide also engages in continuous self-reflection to ensure they remain aligned with the role of a neutral and supportive presence. Self-reflection is a vital practice that allows the guide to examine their own intentions, biases, and emotional responses. This practice cultivates humility, reminding the guide that their role is not one of authority but of accompaniment. Through self-awareness, the guide remains clear and grounded, fully present for the practitioner's needs.

A deep commitment to confidentiality is foundational. Trust is the cornerstone of any therapeutic relationship, and the guide must uphold the practitioner's stories and emotions as sacred and private. In holding confidentiality, the guide honors the vulnerability and trust extended by the practitioner, creating a bond that is secure and respected. This confidentiality strengthens the connection, allowing the practitioner to open fully, knowing their inner world is safeguarded.

In supporting others on the path to rebirth, the guide becomes both witness and companion—a steady presence that honors the practitioner's journey with reverence and respect. It is a role marked not by the guide's own knowledge or insights but by their capacity to hold, support, and reflect. Through this art of guidance, the guide touches the deeper currents of transformation, joining each practitioner in a sacred dance of healing and discovery.

To guide others on the path of liberation and rebirth is to step into the role of a facilitator, a role that demands an alignment of intention, skill, and deep compassion. This journey, both transformative and demanding, calls for tools and techniques that will support not only the practitioner's unique process but also maintain the integrity of the space in which healing unfolds. This chapter delves into the practical application of advanced support techniques, offering a framework for creating an atmosphere that nurtures openness, courage, and profound trust.

Creating an environment of energetic grounding serves as the foundation for a safe and protected space. The guide is encouraged to engage in grounding practices, using breathwork, visualization, and intentional focus to clear their own energy and establish a sense of balance. This personal grounding translates into a calm presence, a steady anchor for the practitioner to rely on, allowing them to relax deeply into their own process.

Guided visualizations can be powerful tools in the guide's repertoire, facilitating deeper exploration of emotions and memories. By carefully crafting imagery that resonates with the practitioner's current needs and challenges, the guide invites them into a reflective space, where symbols and metaphors emerge naturally. This exploration often reveals subconscious insights, unlocking layers of self-awareness that may have been inaccessible through conventional conversation alone. Each visualization should be approached with gentleness, always allowing space for the practitioner's unique interpretations to surface.

Supporting others often requires knowledge of energetic protection techniques to ensure both guide and practitioner remain energetically healthy and aligned. Techniques such as creating a mental shield of light around the space, visualizing a boundary that separates energies, or even symbolic gestures of cleansing—like using water or smoke—can help purify and protect the shared space. These practices reassure both participants, establishing a setting where emotional release and vulnerability can occur without the risk of energetic entanglement.

In moments of intense release, somatic support techniques become essential. The guide can encourage the practitioner to stay connected to their physical experience, guiding them to breathe into areas of tension or even to place their hands over their heart or abdomen to provide a self-soothing anchor. This grounding in the body helps the practitioner remain present, ensuring they navigate their emotional process without feeling overwhelmed or disconnected.

Working with others on this path also introduces the delicate balance of timing and patience. As practitioners explore the depths of their emotional landscapes, the guide must allow silence, offering pauses and creating space for unspoken realizations. These quiet moments can often carry the weight of profound insights, and the guide's patience fosters a trust in the natural unfolding of the practitioner's journey.

For times when a practitioner encounters resistance or fear, gentle encouragement techniques can aid in overcoming these barriers. The guide might offer reminders of the practitioner's inner strength, quietly affirming their capacity to face what arises. Through gentle, validating words, the guide reinforces that discomfort and uncertainty are intrinsic to the growth process. This encouragement is neither forceful nor dismissive; it is a calm presence, reminding the practitioner that they are not alone and that they are indeed capable.

An effective guide will also integrate reflective questioning techniques, which allow the practitioner to examine their own beliefs and assumptions. Instead of providing direct answers, the guide can ask open-ended questions that prompt introspection. Questions such as "What does this experience remind you of?" or "How does this sensation feel in your body?" encourage practitioners to delve deeper into their own responses, uncovering insights that contribute to their liberation and self-awareness.

In fostering the long-term growth of others, integration techniques are essential. After intense sessions or experiences, the guide may offer reflective exercises, such as journaling prompts or suggested meditative practices, to help practitioners process their insights and carry them into daily life. Integration practices ensure that the experiences within the session do not remain isolated but become woven into the fabric of the practitioner's ongoing journey.

Guiding others requires that the facilitator engage in continuous personal development. Regular self-reflection, ongoing education, and periodic supervision with mentors or peers ensure that the guide remains balanced and effective. This commitment to growth helps the guide maintain humility and openness, qualities essential for supporting others with clarity and depth.

Finally, cultivating a sense of closure and gratitude at the end of each session creates a sense of completeness and respect for the journey. The guide may close each session with a brief grounding exercise, a moment of mutual gratitude, or a simple acknowledgment of the courage the practitioner has shown. These closing practices honor the work done and prepare both the practitioner and guide to reenter daily life with a sense of clarity and calm.

As the practitioner's path continues, the guide becomes both a witness and a catalyst, honoring the integrity of each unique journey and fostering an environment where transformation can take root and flourish. Through these techniques, the guide's presence becomes a source of stability and empowerment, one that quietly supports the practitioner as they walk forward on the path to rebirth.

Chapter 31
Rebirth Cycle

The culmination of the liberation and rebirth journey marks a profound threshold, as practitioners transition from the structured path of therapeutic practice into the boundless terrain of daily life. This stage invites reflection, integration, and an honoring of the transformations that have unfolded. It is here, in this space of completion, that practitioners are called to weave the essence of their experiences into the fabric of their lives.

In approaching this moment, a sense of reverence for the journey stands at the forefront. The practitioner, having traversed the depths of self-discovery, must now engage in practices that celebrate and consolidate their growth. Gratitude rituals hold a central place in this process. Simple but powerful, these rituals may include moments of silent reflection, journaling about key insights, or meditative acknowledgments of the inner strength uncovered. These practices deepen the sense of fulfillment and appreciation for each step taken, reinforcing the personal power cultivated throughout the journey.

As this period of closure begins, practitioners often find that the process of self-review offers a profound perspective on their evolution. Looking back on the path—from initial uncertainties to the emergence of new perspectives—can offer both clarity and validation. Questions such as "What fears did I release?" or "Which aspects of my inner self have emerged?" allow practitioners to see the contours of their journey. This reflection reinforces the significance of every experience, small or large, and brings the practitioner into a deeper relationship with the self.

The concept of symbolic closure can also enhance the experience of completion. Just as rituals marked the journey's beginning and its unfolding, they now serve to honor its conclusion. For some, this may mean creating a physical token or symbol that embodies the essence of transformation—a stone, a drawing, or an object from nature. Others may find solace in a ceremonial act, such as lighting a candle or creating a sacred space, that reflects the ending of one phase and the readiness to embrace another. These gestures, however simple, create a bridge from the internal to the external, manifesting the practitioner's growth in a tangible way.

The integration of insights into daily life is both a continuation and a culmination of the journey. Practices of mindful living become essential tools, helping practitioners maintain a steady connection to their inner growth. By approaching routine tasks with intentionality, they transform daily moments into ongoing acts of self-connection. This may involve setting brief intentions for the day, grounding oneself with a moment of stillness, or simply noticing one's emotional state without judgment. These small but intentional acts reinforce the journey's lessons, allowing the insights gained to root deeply within.

As the practitioner begins to reengage with the world, the question of balance and boundaries becomes relevant. Returning to the rhythms of daily life, there is a delicate balance to be struck between maintaining inner tranquility and engaging with the external world. Practices like conscious breathing, self-reflection, and, when needed, gently establishing personal boundaries allow practitioners to protect their inner clarity. With these tools, they can navigate relationships and responsibilities without losing the essence of their transformative experience.

Reaching out to a community or support network serves as another form of closure. Sharing insights and experiences with others who have walked a similar path can offer a sense of kinship and shared understanding. Whether through conversations, group practices, or written reflections, connecting with others fosters an environment of mutual support and encouragement. This network reinforces the idea that while the liberation and rebirth journey may be deeply personal, it is also part of a larger, interconnected human experience.

Throughout this process, practitioners may encounter moments of emotional release, as feelings rise to the surface for final acknowledgment. Acknowledging these emotions without clinging to them allows for a true sense of liberation. Practitioners can engage in grounding practices, such as walking in nature, journaling, or simply sitting in silence to witness the flow of their emotions. Each emotion, no matter how intense, holds meaning, and honoring these sensations completes the cycle of healing with grace.

In bringing this phase of the journey to a close, practitioners may also find strength in visualizing the legacy of their inner work. Imagining the ways in which their growth may influence future interactions, projects, and personal goals serves as a powerful reminder that this journey is not truly ending but evolving. It is the beginning of a new chapter, marked by an expanded sense of self, readiness, and purpose.

The practice of self-compassion becomes a constant companion as practitioners step forward. Recognizing that growth continues in subtle and sometimes unanticipated ways, they can approach life's challenges with gentleness and patience. This compassion fosters resilience, reminding the practitioner that the strength gained throughout the journey is ever-present, awaiting moments when it is most needed.

As this transformative cycle reaches its conclusion, practitioners emerge with a profound sense of completeness, ready to embrace life with newfound clarity and courage. The experiences, insights, and changes achieved during this journey become an integral part of their being, guiding them toward a future illuminated by self-awareness and authentic purpose.

As the final chapter unfolds, practitioners are guided through the sacred act of preserving the journey's profound transformations. Here, the emphasis is on nurturing and maintaining the inner growth achieved, embedding it into a lasting state of well-being and continuous self-discovery.

To begin this phase, practitioners focus on weaving their experiences into a personal philosophy, a deeply individualized set of principles born from the trials, insights, and wisdom of the liberation and rebirth process. By reflecting on how their values have shifted or become clearer, they craft a framework for approaching life's complexities with balance and clarity. This philosophy becomes the lens through which they perceive and respond to both inner and outer challenges. It may emphasize gratitude, forgiveness, inner strength, or a commitment to authenticity—qualities cultivated in the depths of their journey.

The practices of self-knowledge and ongoing self-care take root as essential pillars. Just as the therapeutic journey offered structured practices for growth, this phase encourages practitioners to design a sustainable routine that reflects their unique needs. These practices might include meditative reflections, breathwork, mindful journaling, or regular time in nature. Each serves as a touchstone, a grounding ritual that brings them back to the core of their liberation whenever life feels fragmented or overwhelming.

In preserving the insights gained, awareness of the mind-body connection is paramount. Having journeyed through an intense process of emotional release and energetic realignment, practitioners now understand the importance of listening to the signals of both body and mind. Gentle exercises, stretching, and somatic practices nurture this awareness, helping maintain a harmonious flow of energy. These practices not only reinforce physical vitality but also remind practitioners of the holistic unity within them—a balance cultivated and safeguarded throughout the therapeutic experience.

The concept of periodic renewal is introduced as a means of sustaining the transformation achieved. Life's rhythms and cycles are mirrored in this phase, encouraging practitioners to revisit their rituals at intervals that feel intuitively right. Revisiting breathing techniques, meditation practices, or reflective exercises in these moments of self-renewal provides clarity and maintains the alignment achieved in earlier stages. This periodic return serves as a quiet but powerful affirmation that growth is a lifelong journey, gently renewed with each season, each phase, each new chapter.

Through visualization exercises, practitioners anchor the expanded identity that has emerged. Visualization becomes a powerful tool to align their inner state with future aspirations, blending the insights from their journey with the vision of the life they seek to live. In visualizing interactions, responses, and personal milestones, practitioners cultivate a mental landscape that aligns with their values, empowering them to navigate life with resilience and inner clarity.

The practice of celebrating milestones, however small or personal, becomes an integral part of this final stage. Each significant achievement, no matter how subtle, is honored as a reflection of the practitioner's journey. These celebrations are not grand gestures; rather, they are mindful recognitions—perhaps lighting a candle, expressing gratitude, or quietly acknowledging growth. Such moments solidify the practitioner's bond with their journey, instilling a gentle reminder of how far they have come and how far they will continue to go.

An invitation to redefine success and fulfillment is also central. Freed from old patterns and expectations, practitioners explore what success truly means within their new paradigm of self-understanding. For some, fulfillment may now arise from moments of peace, presence, and connection, rather than external achievements or validation. This redefined sense of success aligns them more deeply with their inner purpose, allowing each choice and action to be imbued with authenticity and intention.

Finally, practitioners are encouraged to contribute their growth to the greater good. Through compassion, active listening, or sharing their experiences with others, they create a ripple effect that extends the essence of their journey beyond themselves. This contribution need not be overt or directed—it may simply be the influence of their calm presence, the quiet strength they carry, or the empathy they offer to others. In these subtle yet impactful ways, practitioners continue to embody the healing and liberation they have experienced.

As this journey concludes, practitioners stand not at an ending but at the threshold of a continually unfolding path. They are equipped with practices, insights, and an inner resilience that illuminate the way forward. With this final chapter, the essence of their journey becomes a steady presence, a quiet and enduring source of strength, as they step into life with purpose, clarity, and an open heart.

Epilogue

As you reach the end of this work, perhaps you realize that what you found here was more than you expected, and less than you thought you understood. But do not be mistaken: this is only the beginning of a path without end, a road that unfolds far beyond the pages you have just read. What now echoes in your mind, the revelations that have unfolded within your spirit, are seeds that will germinate throughout your life, shaping the way you see yourself and the universe around you.

The rebirth you experienced here is not a singular event but a continuous process, a flow that invites you to dive ever deeper into your own essence. What you left behind—fears, pains, old beliefs—was necessary to make room for the new, for what now reveals itself within you. But this empty space is only the fertile ground where new growth begins, where new perspectives and visions of the world take root.

Perhaps you have come to understand that the answers are not outside, but in the silence that dwells within, in the pauses between one thought and another. And, in truth, there are no definitive answers. There is only the constant movement of your being, which adapts, transforms, and frees itself with each new cycle. What was once pain now becomes understanding. What was once resistance now transforms into acceptance.

This book, therefore, is a guide, a companion on the journey that, at some point, will also need to be set aside. Because the true journey happens beyond the words, in the encounters you will have with yourself, in the nights of doubt and the days of discovery. And, when those moments arrive, you will know that you are no longer alone. The essence of what you have learned here will remain with you, like a gentle breeze reminding you of your own capacity to be reborn.

Look around you and realize that everything, just like you, is in constant transformation. Nature, time, the stars that sparkle in the sky. And you, as part of this great mystery, are also reborn at every moment. May you, from this point forward, embrace each cycle of change with the certainty that there is always something greater guiding you, a flow that, though invisible, pulses in harmony with the rhythm of your own breath.

Now, with a lighter heart and awakened spirit, remember that what you carry within is a reflection of the universe, and that each step you take on this new journey is an invitation to the unknown, an invitation to the expansion of all you thought you were. And so, as you close this book, may you feel not an end but a new beginning, an opportunity to explore what you are in depth, without fear, without reservations.

This is the gift that remains: the possibility to live fully, to find beauty in the simplicity of being, to recognize that true awakening resides in each choice you make, in each breath you take. And thus, continue on your journey, knowing that the cycle of rebirth never truly ends, but only expands, inviting you to be always more, to be fully yourself.

Luiz Santos

www.ingramcontent.com/pod-product-compliance
Lightning Source LLC
La Vergne TN
LVHW040143080526
838202LV00042B/3007